Ron... u

MW01252360

the POWER
of the Cross

A MUSICAL PRAISING CHRIST, THE RISEN LAMB

MARTY PARKS

easy 2 excel

lillenas
PUBLISHING COMPANY

lillenas.com

Alphabetical Index

Contents in Sequence

A Call to Praise

includes
Creation Overture
All the Earth
We Will Worship the Lamb of Glory

Arr. by Marty Parks

**WORSHIP LEADER: Shout to the Lord, all the earth! Worship Him with
gladness; come before Him with your singing. God's Word says that
He inhabits the praises of His people, so clap your hands everyone;
and shout to God with your cries of joy! How awesome He is–the Lord
Most High. He's the Creator of heaven and earth. Enthroned in splendor
and majesty, He is God alone. And this earth will be filled with the knowledge of His glory, just as the waters cover the sea. So, be exalted, O God,
above the heavens, and now, even now, let Your glory be over all the earth!
(adapted from Psa. 100:1,2; Psa. 47:1,2; Isa. 37:16; Hab. 2:14 and Psa. 57:5)

Acoustic rock ♩ = ca. 92

6

CD: 3

Lord, Be - fore You,___ all life a -

dores You. All the earth___ will de - clare___ that Your love

is ev - 'ry - where;___ The fields will___ ex - alt,

9

CD: 4 *1st time*

glo - ri - fy and bless Your ho - ly___ name!

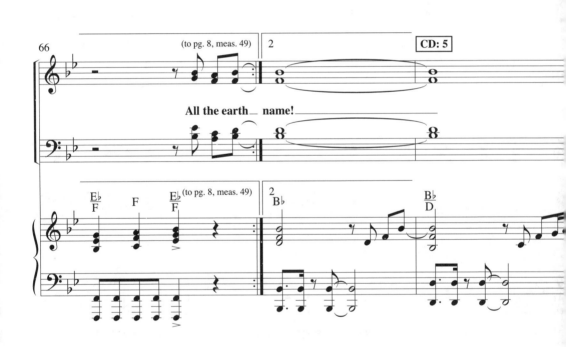

(to pg. 8, meas. 49)

CD: 5

All the earth___ name!

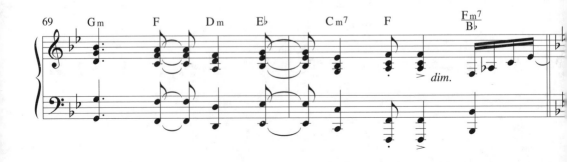

*"We Will Worship the Lamb of Glory"

SOLO *with freedom*
(or Choir unis.)

We will wor-ship the Lamb____ of glo - ry,

We will wor-ship the King____ of kings;____

We will wor-ship the Lamb____ of glo - ry,

We will wor-ship the King.____

16

All the Earth Will Sing Your Praises

Words and Music by
PAUL BALOCHE
Arr. by Marty Parks

20

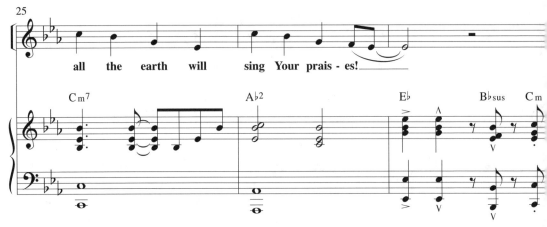

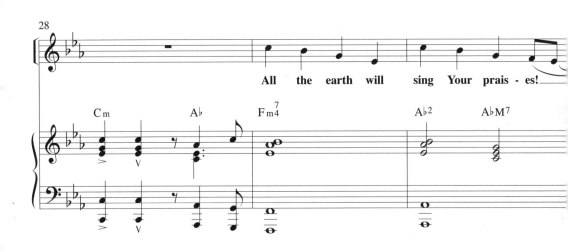

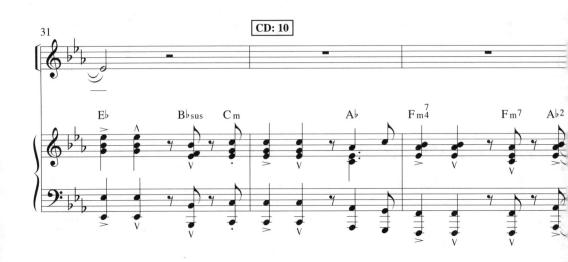

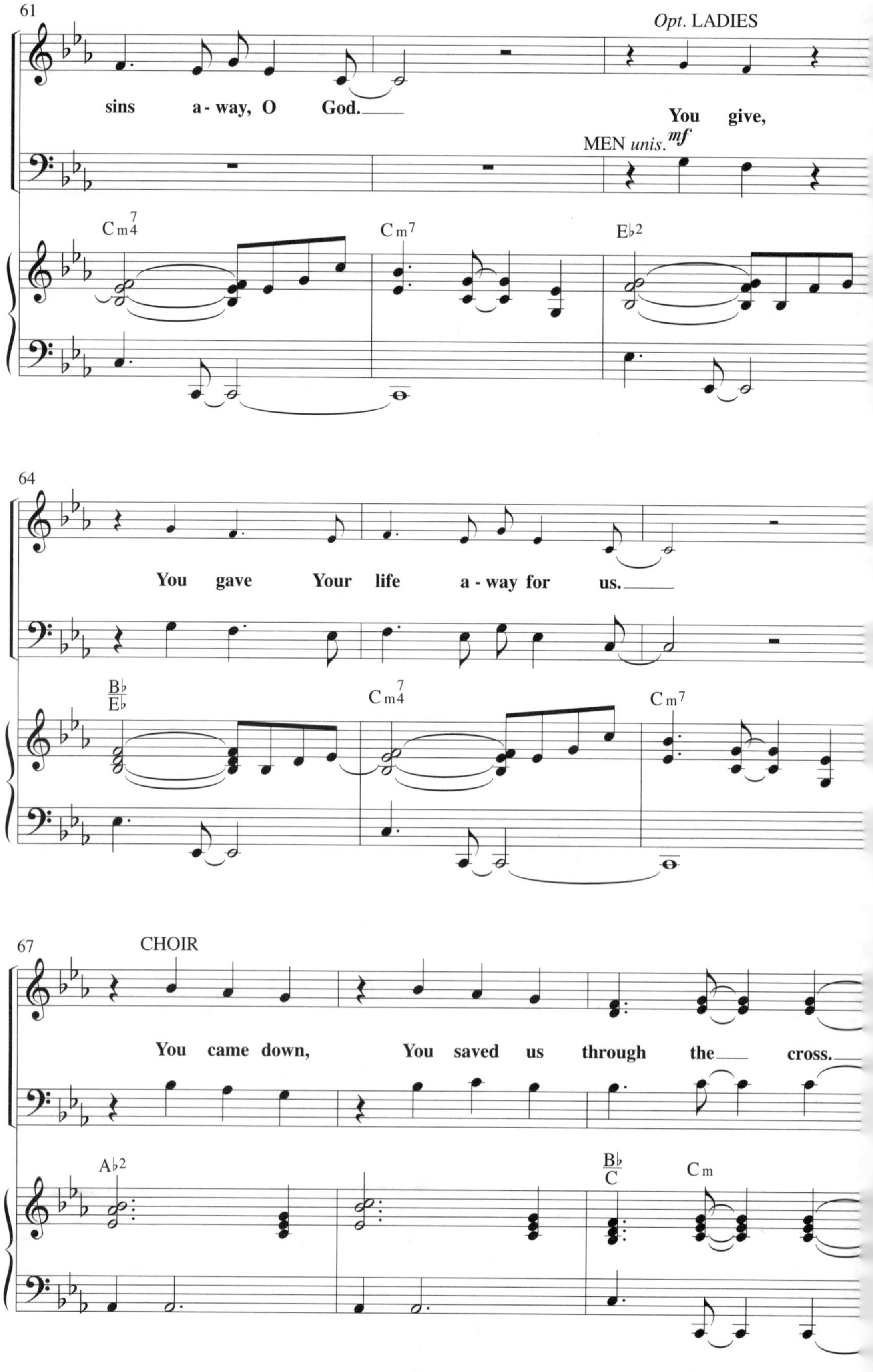

61
Opt. LADIES
sins a - way, O God.
You give,
MEN unis. mf
Cm4 7
Cm7
E♭2
64
You gave Your life a - way for us.
B♭/E♭
Cm4 7
Cm7
67
CHOIR
You came down, You saved us through the cross.
A♭2
B♭/C
Cm

27

WORSHIP LEADER *(without music)*: Oh, yes! All the earth *will* sing
His praises! You see, our worship, even right now in this place,
is our response to God–for all He is, and for all He's done.

(Music begins)

God Gave

Underscore

MARTY PARKS
Arr. by Marty Parks

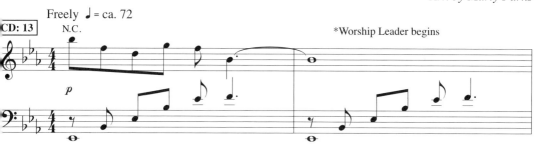

*WORSHIP LEADER: Think for a moment about these words,
   God gave . . . God gave.
For those looking for purpose and direction,
   God gave a Wonderful Counselor.
For those filled with anxiety and strife,
   God gave a Prince of Peace.
To the lost and helpless,
   God gave a Good Shepherd.
To those needing a voice in their brokenness,
   God gave an Advocate.
And for all those who have no one to identify with in their
   suffering and pain, God gave a Man of Sorrows.
To those seeking answers,
   the Truth.
To the ones ravaged by physical illness and spiritual calamity,
   the Great Physician.
And for all of those facing the darkness of death,
   God gave the Resurrection and the Life.
And as if that weren't enough, to everyone with no spark of divine
   presence in their lives, He gave Immanuel–God with us.

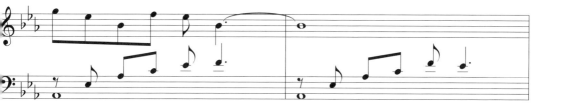

Unfailing Love

with
Fairest Lord Jesus

Words and Music by
CHRIS TOMLIN, ED CASH
and CAREY PIERCE
Arr. by Marty Parks

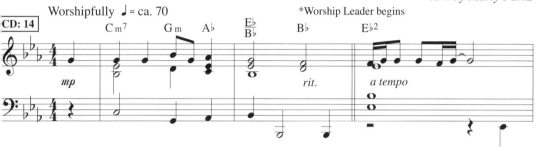

*WORSHIP LEADER: God loved the world so much–
He loved you so much–that He gave us . . . His Son.*

Yours for - ev - er. You are my strength, God of grace and mer - cy. And ev - 'ry-thing____ You hold in Your hand, Still You make And ev - 'ry-thing,____

nev - er change; God, You re-main__ the Ho - ly One,__ And my un - fail - ing

love, un - fail - ing__ love._____

CD: 16 *1st time*
CD: 18 *2nd time*

2nd time to Coda ⊕
(to pg. 36, meas. 36)

2nd time to Coda ⊕
(to pg. 36, meas. 36)

SOLO *with freedom*
mf

You are__ my_____ Rock, the One I

38

Mighty Is the Power of the Cross

Words and Music by
CHRIS TOMLIN, SHAWN CRAIG
and JESSE REEVES
Arr. by Marty Parks

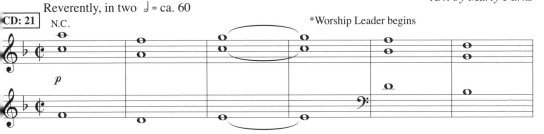

*WORSHIP LEADER: Only God would choose to show us triumph
through tragedy, hope through disaster and life through death.
Whatever you're going through, my friend, He's with you right
now to bring you through. O Father, thank You for the life-
changing, undeniable, mighty power of the cross.

CHOIR *unis.*
(Opt. Solo 1st time)

1. What can take a dy - ing man,
2. What re - stores our faith in God?

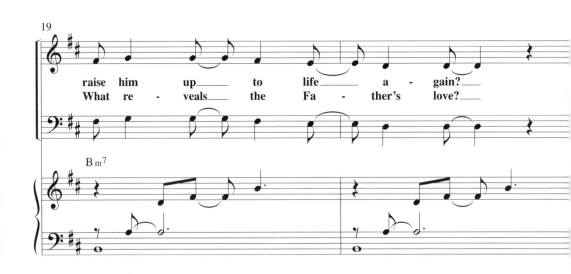

raise him up to life a - gain?
What re - veals the Fa - ther's love?

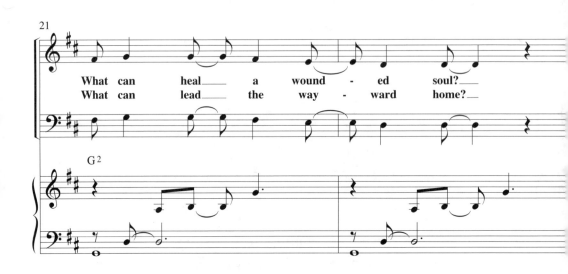

What can heal a wound - ed soul?
What can lead the way - ward home?

What can make us white as snow?
What can melt a heart of stone?

A/G♯

CHOIR *div.*
(Opt. Duet 1st time)

What can fill the emp - ti - ness?
What can free the guilt - y ones?

D²

What can mend our bro - ken - ness,
What can save and o - ver - come,

B m⁷

44

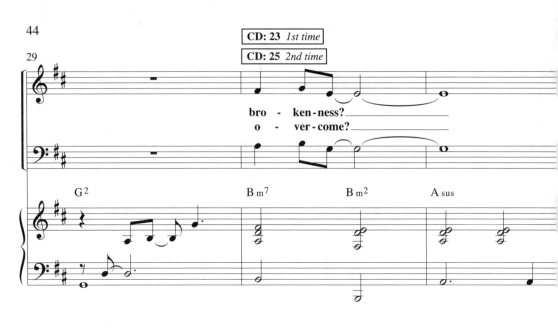

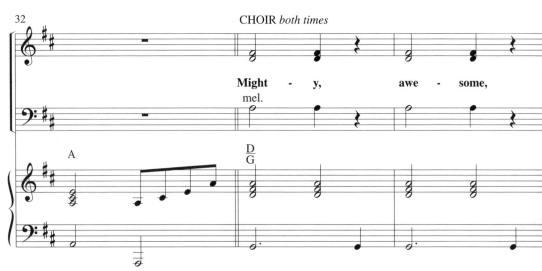

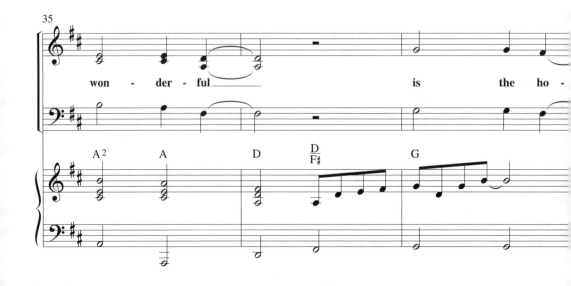

46

83

mf

Where the Lamb laid down His life

86

to lift us from the fall.

89

Might - y

Might - y is

pow - er   of   the   cross!

WORSHIP LEADER *(without music)*: It seems inconceivable,
even hideous to us now that Jesus, the Lord of Glory, would
willingly subject Himself to betrayal, torture and finally death
on a shameful cross. As His beloved disciple, John, would later
write, *He is the atoning sacrifice for our sins, and not only for
ours but also for the sins of the whole world. (1 John 2:2* NIV)

You remember the story, don't you? Jesus and His disciples had
just finished the Passover meal, His last meal with them. As He
began to speak to them of things to come–His betrayal and His
death–a heavy spirit of despair filled the room. Suddenly, Judas,
the one who would hand Him over to the religious authorities,
fled the room and escaped . . . into the shadow of darkness.

(Music begins)

The Hour of Shadows

Underscore

MARTY PARKS
Arr. by Marty Parks

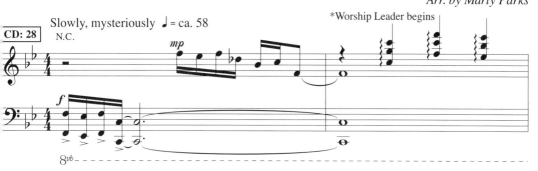

*WORSHIP LEADER: Then Jesus, with His remaining followers, left the upper
room and entered a garden close by. He told them to watch and pray while
He went a little distance from them. His hour had come, and as He began to
speak to His Father, the weight of all the sins of the world fell on Him like the
blackness of the night. Yes, for the Savior of the world, it was the hour of shadows.

VOICE 1: Then Judas, together with a large crowd from the chief priests and
elders of the people, burst into the garden, shattering its sacred silence.

VOICE 2: They were armed with swords and clubs, and were looking for Jesus.

VOICE 1: Judas approached his Master and kissed Him, indicating to the mob
the One they were after.

VOICE 2: They arrested Him, and dragged Him back to Jerusalem to appear
before Caiphas, the high priest. They accused Him of blasphemy and treason.

VOICE 1: They sent Him to Pilate, the Roman governor, where again He was
questioned, mocked and ridiculed.

VOICE 2: He was slapped, beaten and spit on.

VOICE 1: He was deserted and disowned.

VOICE 2: He was insulted and abandoned.

VOICE 1: He was not crowned the King of Glory,

VOICE 2: But He was sentenced to a criminal's death!

WORSHIP LEADER *(without music)*: Finally, Pilate handed Him over to the
people; and He was led out to be crucified.

"Worship Leader: . . .
the hour of shadows."

CD: 29   "Voice 1: Then Judas . . ."

Faster, agitated ♩ = ca. 132

Segue to "Here I Am to Worship"

Here I Am to Worship

with

When I Survey the Wondrous Cross

Words and Music by
TIM HUGHES
Arr. by Marty Park

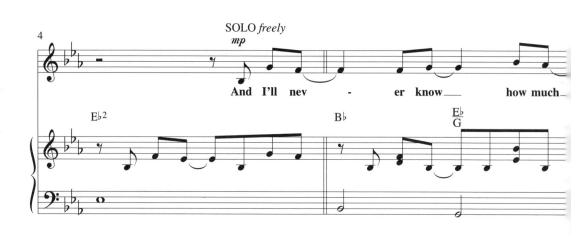

CD: 31

Simply ♩ = ca. 74

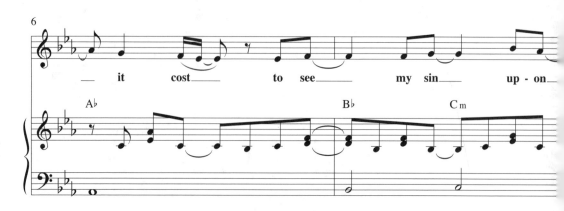

PLEASE NOTE: Copying of this product is NOT covered by CCLI licenses. For CCLI information call 1-800-234-2446

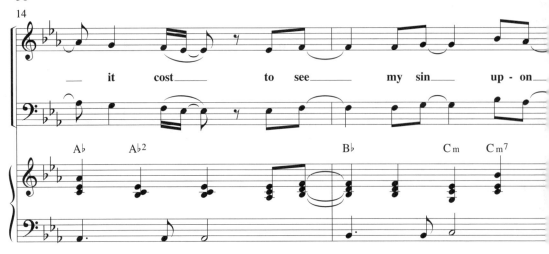

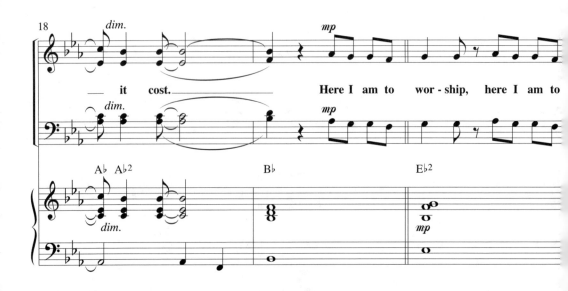

60

You're al-to-geth-er love-ly, al-to-geth-er wor-thy; Al-to-geth-er won-der-ful to me!

CD: 34

*"When I Survey the Wondrous Cross"

Were the whole realm of

*WORSHIP LEADER: Then Jesus cried out in a loud
voice, "Father, into Your hands I commit My spirit.
It . . . is . . . finished."

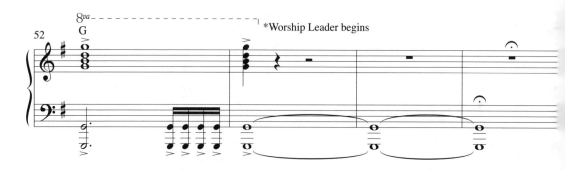

What Wondrous Love Is This

merican Folk Hymn

William Walker's *Southern Harmony*
Arr. by Marty Parks

1st time: LADIES unis.
2nd time: MEN unis. (or Choir unis.)

1. What won-drous love is this, O my
(2. When) I was sink - ing down, sink - ing

soul, O my soul! What won - drous love is
down, sink - ing soul down, When I was sink - ing

this,   O my   soul!   What

down,   sink - ing down,   When

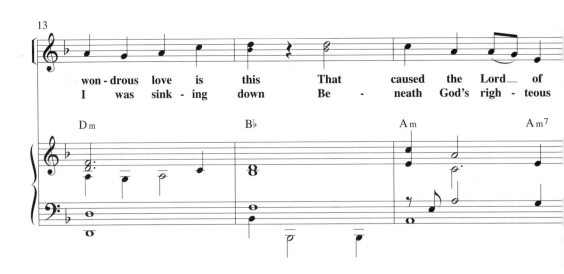

won - drous love   is   this   That   caused   the Lord__ of

I   was sink - ing down   Be -   neath God's righ - teous

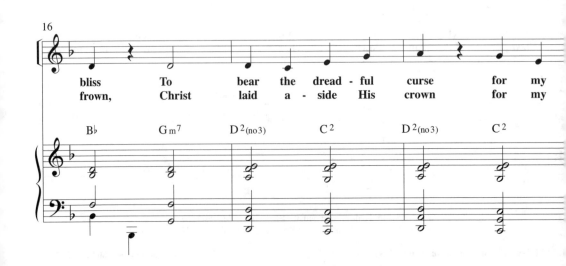

bliss   To   bear the dread - ful curse   for   my

frown,   Christ   laid a - side   His crown   for   my

sing! To God and to the

Lamb Who is the great I AM! While

mil - lions join the theme, I will sing, I will

68

Behold the Lamb

Underscore

MARTY PARKS
Arr. by Marty Parks

*Worship Leader begins

*WORSHIP LEADER: He was led like a lamb to slaughter, and as a sheep before her shearers is silent, so He did not open His mouth. *(Isa. 53:7 NIV)* Behold the Lamb of God–the Lamb who takes away our sins; the Lamb slain before the foundation of the world; the Lamb worthy of glory and honor and praise; the Lamb now enthroned in heaven at His Father's right hand. For death could not keep Him and the grave could not contain Him.

Behold! Jesus Christ, the Risen Lamb!

Hallelujah, the Lamb Is Alive!

MARTY PARKS and
CHARLES WESLEY

MARTY PARKS
Arr. by Marty Parks

72

Christ the Lord___ is ris'n___ to - day;___

Hal - le - lu - jah the Lamb___ is a - live!___ Sons of men___ and an -

- gels___ say:___ Hal - le - lu - jah the Lamb___ is a - live!___

74

WORSHIP LEADER *(without music)*: O yes! The Lamb *IS* alive!

82

The Song of the Redeemed

includes

He Reigns
All the Earth

Arr. by Marty Par

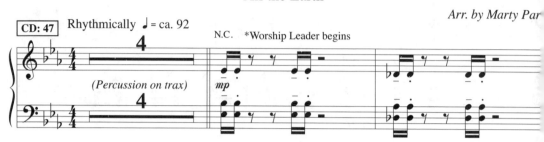

*WORSHIP LEADER: The Lamb who with His blood purchased us for God from every tribe, language, people and nation. And from every corner of the earth, the song of the redeemed can be heard. It resounds from jungles and deserts, and from mountains and cities. It echoes from small gatherings of believers and from multitudes of the faithful. Their song is the song of the Lamb– *Hallelujah! For the Lord God Almighty Reigns! (Rev. 19:6 NIV)*

Medley © 2007 by PsalmSinger Music (BMI). All rights reserved.
Administered by The Copyright Company, PO Box 128139, Nashville, TN 37212-8139.

85

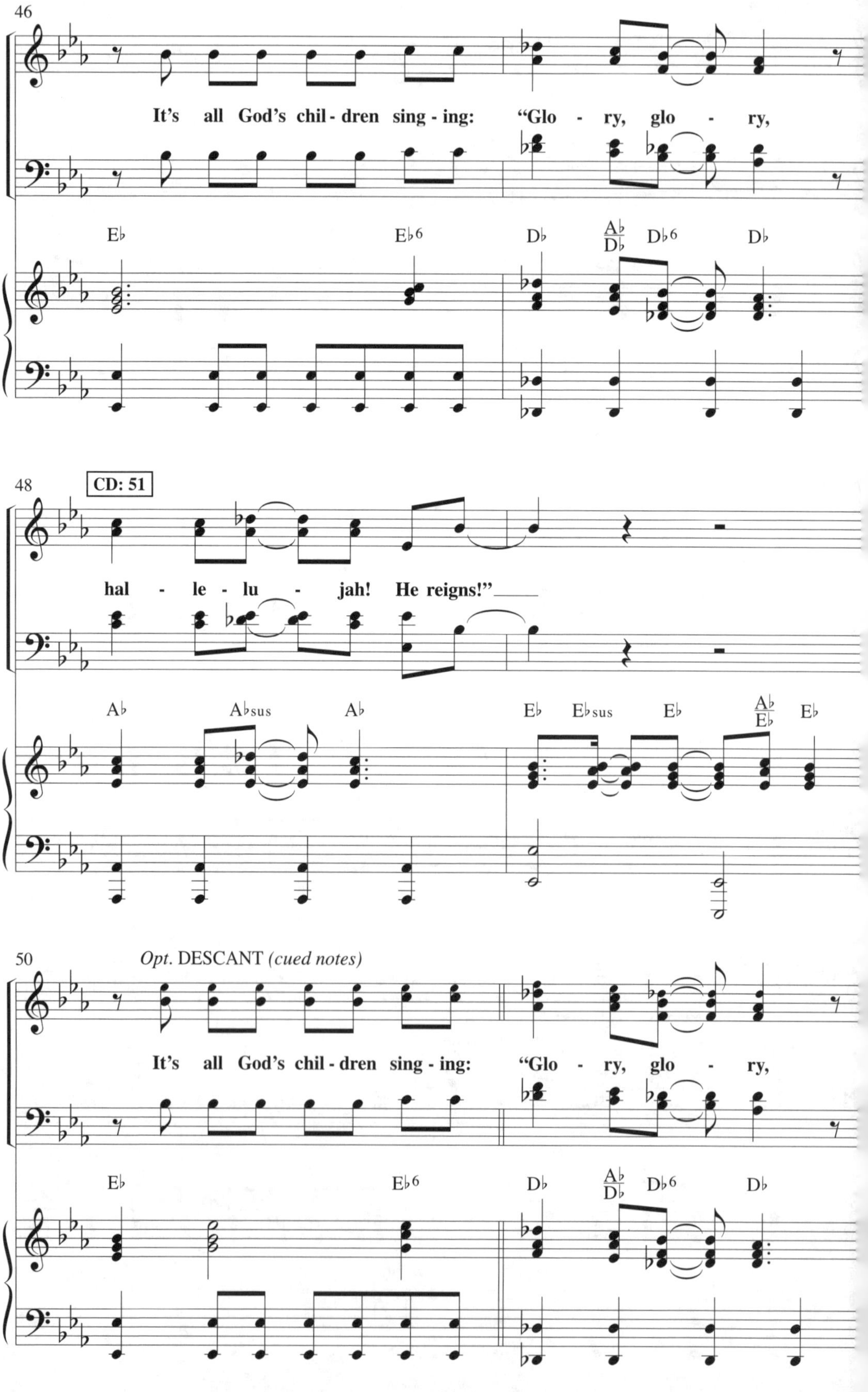

46
It's all God's chil - dren sing - ing: "Glo - ry, glo - ry,
E♭ E♭6 D♭ A♭/D♭ D♭6 D♭
48
CD: 51
hal - le - lu - jah! He reigns!"
A♭ A♭sus A♭ E♭ E♭sus E♭ A♭/E♭ E♭
50
Opt. DESCANT (cued notes)
It's all God's chil - dren sing - ing: "Glo - ry, glo - ry,
E♭ E♭6 D♭ A♭/D♭ D♭6 D♭

91

70
Hear the trees joy - ful cry,
Eb/F F Eb/F F Bb Bbsus/C
72
prais - ing You; and so will I!
Bb/D F7sus F Gm F
74
A new song I'll sing;
Eb Bb/D

93

LA...
LEARNS BEST
LEARNS MOST

TO LIVE
THE IMPOSSIBLE DREAM
IS TO WORK FOR
PADUL-OH!

LIFE IS BEAUTIFUL
THEN YOU GO TO
HEAVEN

IN THE PADULO BUILDING

I CAN GET IT FOR YOU RETAIL

Down and Dirty Tales from a Canadian Ad Man

Rick Padulo

DUNDURN
TORONTO

Editor: Donald G. Bastian, Bastian Publishing Services Ltd.
Interior design: Tony Bove; Daniel Crack, Kinetics Design
Cover design: Pat Lore; Daniel Crack, Kinetics Design, www.kdbooks.ca
Illustrations on page 54 and 59: Tony Bove
Printer: Transcontinental

Library and Archives Canada Cataloguing in Publication

Padulo, Rick
    I can get it for you retail : down and dirty tales from a Canadian ad man / Rick Padulo.

Includes index.
Issued also in electronic formats.
ISBN 978-1-4597-0500-5

    1. Padulo, Rick. 2. Advertising executives – Canada – Biography. I. Title.

HF5810.P33A3 2012   659.1092   C2012-900072-8

1   2   3   4   5   16   15   14   13   12

| Conseil des Arts du Canada | Canada Council for the Arts | | ONTARIO ARTS COUNCIL CONSEIL DES ARTS DE L'ONTARIO |

We acknowledge the support of the **Canada Council for the Arts** and the **Ontario Arts Council** for our publishing program. We also acknowledge the financial support of the **Government of Canada** through the **Canada Book Fund** and **Livres Canada Books**, and the **Government of Ontario** through the **Ontario Book Publishing Tax Credit** and the **Ontario Media Development Corporation**.

Care has been taken to trace the ownership of copyright material used in this book. The author and the publisher welcome any information enabling them to rectify any references or credits in subsequent editions.

J. Kirk Howard, President

Printed and bound in Canada.
www.dundurn.com

Dundurn	Gazelle Books Services Limited	Dundurn
3 Church Street, Suite 500	White Cross Mills	2250 Military Road
Toronto, Ontario, Canada	High Town, Lancaster, England	Tonawanda, NY
M5E 1M2	LA1 4XS	U.S.A. 14150

CONTENTS

DEDICATION

In Loving Memory of

Charles Alexander Padulo.

'ALEX'

November 14, 1982 – April 6, 2006

Not a day goes by that we don't think of you.

Love, Dad

OUR INVENTORY GOES UP AND DOWN THE ELEVATOR EVERY DAY

My Human Resources philosophy can best be summed up in a phrase that I coined ... it relates to the fact that I'm always looking for people who can think for themselves and also operate as part of a team.

I'M LOOKING FOR EAGLES THAT CAN FLY IN FORMATION!

Dad Frank, Mother Norma, and me. They're gone now
but I know they're watching over me.

Big brother Jos (pronounced "Joe") with
me in front of the Padulo Building.

PROLOGUE

LIFE is good and then you go to heaven and even though there have been some very dark days in my life that's pretty much the attitude I've carried throughout my career.

My parents Norma and Frank taught me so much but most of all they loved me unconditionally. Their love shaped my life. That was my "normal" and I was so blessed to have them and my big brother Jos always looking out for me.

I love people and for the most part people love me. I've lived a life filled with laughter, joy, and celebration.

Through it all I've spent my business life always trying to do the right thing and I have always placed each client's best interest ahead of my own.

I've found that I can always find something that will give my clients an edge. The relentless pursuit to uncover that edge for them is what keeps me up at night but it's also what excites and drives me.

The edge can manifest itself in different ways but when you hit on it (and you always know when you have) you must leverage the hell out of it with fanatical zeal – and with retail, instant gratification just isn't fast enough.

Good retail and good retailers move quickly – they have a sense of urgency. I remember working as a baby account guy with a client in the retail shmata business. We were working on a particularly aggressive campaign and I said, perhaps a tad sarcastically, "I suppose you want to see the campaign tomorrow."

"No, smart guy, if I wanted it tomorrow I would have asked for it tomorrow," he snapped.

It was one of the most teachable moments in my life: In true retail style, he wanted me to get everything done that very day.

Welcome to the world of retail!

I think most people will find *I Can Get It for You Retail* a quirky read. It's part personal memoir, part chronicle of survival, and part a how-to of retail marketing based on Rick's Nine Commandments.

One thing this book is not, is airy-fairy. I started in the business four decades ago and as Al Pacino says in *Scent of a Woman*, "I've seen some things, you know."

So I'm not going to talk theory. I'm going to talk about real people, real-life events, and real-life adventures and misadventures. I'm going to use actual campaign case studies like Black's Is Photography; Leon's – Don't Pay a Cent Event; Zellers – Because ... the Lowest Price Is the Law; CIBC – Seeing Beyond; and Rexall – A Pharmacy First. However, I'm going to talk about the case studies in an unconventional manner. I'm going to talk about them in a profoundly personal way because in the end it was the people coupled with the methodology that created the success.

So this book is very personal to me, but as the King of Jingle Syd Kessler said to me, "Rick, your public persona is not who you are; your book has got to, among other things, show who you are."

My old boss, mentor, and dear friend Morris Saffer said in an article in *Marketing* magazine, "Padulo's earnestness is unfairly mistaken for swagger. Retail and advertising is a relentless taskmaster, and if you can't maintain that enthusiasm, day in and day out, regardless of all the elements conspiring to defeat you, you can't survive. And Rick is, above all else, a great survivor."

The truth is I just would not still be standing if I didn't have an element of that street-fighting, swaggering, entrepreneurial spirit. I'd like to pretend that things have come easy to me (because you never want to let people see you sweat) but nothing has. I guess I'm a bit of a dichotomy because my mother Norma infused me with both a fighting spirit and a marshmallow heart. I'm in constant "identity crisis mode." So it's a weird combination – maniac and marshmallow – but somehow it has worked for me.

On the marshmallow side, every morning I wake up thinking of the people who work for us and their families and the vendors we deal with and their families. I think about the heartache of losing a piece of business and the people it affects. The most painful part of it is the helplessness you feel. We have never lost a piece of business for cause. The only times we have lost some business were when:

- *There was a management change (on the client side).*
- *The client was bought or sold.*
- *The client's procurement people got involved.*

I sometimes liken procurement people in business to Internal Affairs people in a police department – you have to watch them. In procurement the focus is often on cutting not building. I challenge the captains of industry to be vigilant as this process unfolds in a world focused on quarterly results and to take care that short-term gain does not lead to long-term pain. There is a revolution going on out there – just witness the protests on Wall Street and all over the world. I like to think of this revolution as capitalism with a conscience finding a collective voice.

That said, everybody in business gets it. We have got to do things faster, better, cheaper, but our own people must not be penalized for being good at what they do. I do believe in zero-based planning. I do believe that often if it's not broken you can still make it better. But people are not line items. They are living, breathing human beings with families.

Your reputation, your internal and partner relationships, and how you are perceived in the market should be non-negotiable. Remember, perception is reality. People are everybody's business. Do the right thing!

Doug Moen, Padulo Integrated's original creative director, once wrote this line for a CIBC television commercial: "When you never forget where you came from, you can see more clearly where you're going." I think that's true and that's why I'm going to write about some history and also some things happening right now because I often joke that in our business "you're as good as you were tomorrow."

There are no major successes in our business that are not part of a team effort. However, I will tell you that for any campaigns or preemptive positionings I write about in the following pages, I led the team and was the chief architect of their creation.

I will also tell you that every one of these highly successful campaigns had one thing in common: great clients. Great clients really do get great work.

Through it all it's been a hell of a ride with the good far outweighing the bad – and we're not done yet!

That said, I'd be remiss if I didn't start this book by acknowledging that I owe so much to so many clients, friends, and colleagues and l thank you all from the bottom of my heart.

CIBC Corporate Brand TV – "Klondike"

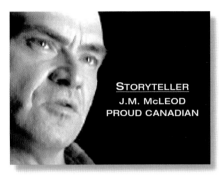

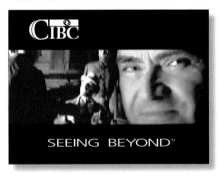

When you never forget where you came from, you can see more clearly where you're going.

As in the past CIBC will continue to play a pioneering role by investing in Canada's vision of the future.

A bank that doesn't see the world through its own eyes, but the eyes of its customers.

A bank that sees what they see and beyond.

WE CAN NEVER, EVER, EVER, THANK OUR CLIENTS ENOUGH

A painting by Nikola Nikola, which is part of a collection that hangs in the Frank P. Padulo Gallery in the Padulo Building.

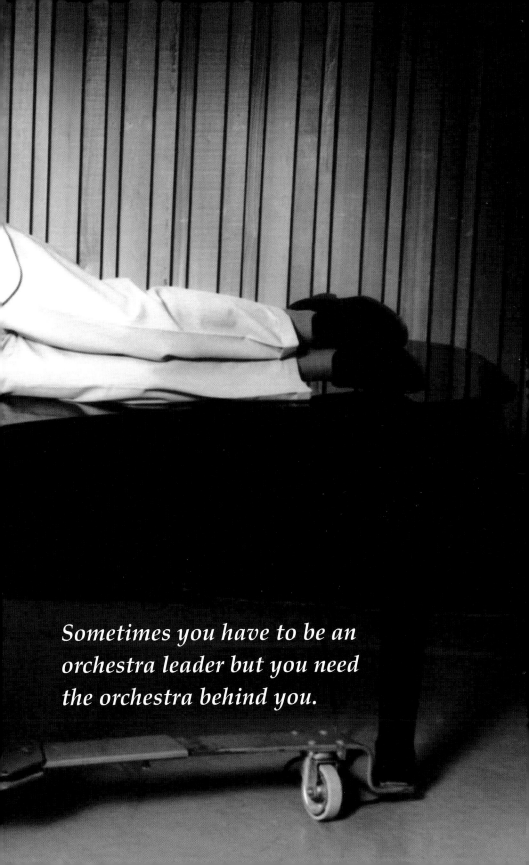

Sometimes you have to be an orchestra leader but you need the orchestra behind you.

With my dad and my big brother Jos.

Steve Hudson and me marlin fishing.

CHAPTER 1

MODEST BEGINNINGS

MY first job in advertising couldn't have been more modest. At sixteen while still in high school I started doing some work as a research assistant for my big brother Jos, who had a small boutique agency in Montreal, the city where we were born and raised. My first job was to hand out questionnaires in Westmount Square, tally the responses, and write a report.

Later, when my brother won the account, he told me that the win was based largely on insights from my report. We had beat out three other agencies and I was euphoric.

From that moment I was hooked on the high of winning new business.

My dear friend Steve Hudson says, "In this world there are hunters and there are gatherers – and only three percent are hunters. You, my brother from a different mother, are a hunter!"

Some years later Jos and I met Morris Saffer, whom we knew as the retail-advertising guru from Toronto. We were introduced by a mutual client, Neil Whitworth, the creative director of Eaton's department store. Morris was doing work for Horizon, the discount store division of Eaton's. My brother, a talented singer/musician/producer, was creating jingles for Eaton's as well as co-hosting and producing a TV show in Montreal sponsored by Eaton's called *Like Young*, and all this while doing post-graduate work in psychology at the University of Montreal.

There was an immediate chemistry between the three of us. Jos, who is ten years older than me, is the same age as Morris. The two of them hit it off as friendly contemporaries. I was the little brother/schlepper/baby account guy who would actually do the grunt work for Morris's Quebec business, Saffer Cravit & Freedman (SCF), working out of my brother's beautiful offices in Youville Stables in Old Montreal.

In those days, especially in Montreal, advertising and life were a party. The best thing about a business trip to Toronto was the plane ride home. We called it Toronto the Boring: bad restaurants, bad theatre, and bad nightlife. Hell, they stopped serving booze at midnight. In Montreal we worked our asses off but we partied. My brother was paying me slave wages (less than his secretary was earning) but I got even by spending a lot on my expense account, a bad habit I cheerfully practice to this day.

As Morris's business in Montreal and my involvement in it continued to grow, the dynamics of the relationship evolved. One thing led to another and we all agreed that it was time for me to spread my wings. Saffer Cravit & Freedman of Toronto hired me to start the Montreal office of their agency.

What a hoot! Suddenly I'm a kid with a cheque book and my own boss – well, kind of (both big brothers were still watching) but there I was out renting a brownstone in downtown Montreal on Dorchester Street: I'm buying furniture, hiring staff, working sixteen hours a day, seven days a week, and having the time of my life. Hell, I did everything – out of necessity: I wrote copy and did the media planning, buying, and account work. I even helped in the graphic art studio. In those days you cut type and cemented it down on boards with a roller. I almost sliced off my index finger with an exacto-knife while trimming a board with a little too much gusto. By the time I was twenty-four I had SCF's Montreal office humming. I was landing new business and generating profits. Life was good.

But in November 1976 somebody "moved our cheese." René Lévesque's separatist party was elected to government in Quebec. Not long after that I relocated to Toronto and two-thirds of my closest friends including two francophones followed suit, landing in Toronto or various other North American cities. It wasn't that a separatist government coming into power meant we had to speak French, because we all could. It was the realization that the province would be left behind the rest of the country. Head office after head office moved out. There was a joke that soon the only document of any social import left in Montreal would be Mayor Drapeau's marriage certificate. For many of us it was a time both of sadness as we uprooted our lives and joy as we made new beginnings.

I wound down the Montreal office and moved to Toronto to work at Saffer Cravit & Freedman's head office and what a ride it was. With Morris Saffer, Don Freedman, and David Cravit at the helm the company was growing like mad. I was still working my sixteen-hour days and weekends but it wasn't working, it was playing because I loved what I was doing with a passion.

It wasn't long after this (while I was still in my twenties) that I was made Senior VP, Client Services. When I first started in the role everyone who worked in client services was older than me. In fact I think I was the youngest person ever appointed to this position in a top ten agency in Canada.

In the end I spent twelve wonderful years in Montreal and Toronto attached to SCF. Lots of exciting things happened to me and around me. Morris Saffer, who was the father of retail advertising in Canada, was at times tough to work with but the angst was worth it. I loved him and still do although I think I still hold the record for the most times anyone was fired by him.

I saw Morris recently at a Saffer reunion. He doesn't remember firing me but we were so close I guess he remembers only the good things, as I must admit do I.

Morris was a driving force. He was passionate, wore his heart on his sleeve, and always wanted the best for his clients. Our mutual desire to succeed resulted in toe-to-toe battles on more than one occasion, which led Don Freedman to comment once, "Padulo, the thing I like most about you is that every time you walk into our offices you're prepared to lose your job." And I really was.

I used to joke that what they really liked most about me was the fact that I was the only one of us in the office on the High Holidays.

The chemistry between us was incredible. I believe that one of the reasons for this was that there is no difference between a Yiddisha mama and an Italian mama. Italians and Jews both love family and food - and know guilt.

One of my best friends in life is David Steinberg, the very talented and famous Canadian comedian/actor/director

With David Steinberg (middle) and Richard Simmons
at a Simmons Mattress TV shoot.

who has lived in Los Angeles for years. David is famous for his involvement with Second City, *The Tonight Show with Johnny Carson*, and *The David Steinberg Show*. He has directed many hit movies, as well as such TV shows as *Seinfeld, Friends, Mad About You*, and *Curb Your Enthusiasm*. He has also directed many TV commercials for me, the first being for Simmons Mattress because David was the only director who could handle Richard Simmons. We actually formed a production company together called Padulo/Steinberg to do small movies.

Anyway, David had the funniest take that I'd ever heard on Jews and Italians and why we get along so well. He once told me that "Italians are just happy Jews" and it's a line that I've shared with all of my Jewish friends. Ronnie Bresler, another of the dearest people in my life, doesn't say hello when he sees my name on his call display. He says, "How's the happy Jew?"

But along with the fun there was substance to my relationship with Saffer Cravit & Freedman. I suppose I was most

Me and my buddy Ron Bresler the day he married the lovely Erin.
Ron has an uncanny ability to be there when you need him.

like Morris in character and that's why we understood each other so well, but there was so much more. Don Freedman, the elder statesman, taught me the most. He spent hours filling me in on retail and leadership skills. He prepped me for meetings and then sent me in as the lead. He built my knowledge, my professional skills, and my confidence, and taught me a lot about dealing with people. Don had little ego and was delighted to groom me so he could steal away to Cape Cod every weekend.

David Cravit had the purest brain among the bunch of us. He was Mensa smart. I always said if I had David's brain I would throw mine away.

Interestingly, I became the go-to guy at SCF. People were leery of going to Morris because he intimidated them. Don was happy to let me be a buffer so he could travel worry free. David never really wanted to deal with the people issues. He could write ads for an entire campaign across all media in the time it took most people to go to lunch and I'm not kidding about that. So in retrospect I can see it was worth a lot more to the company to have David do the writing rather than lunch with a disgruntled creative person who thought the suits (account executives) were disorganized assholes and try to convince them otherwise. I, on the other hand, could get these people kissing in the halls. I always loved people and that made this part of my job easy.

So here I was a little third-generation Italian kid from Montreal being given this enormous opportunity and I grabbed it. They gave me as much rope as I wanted, and although I came close at times I somehow managed never to hang myself.

Saffer Cravit & Freedman helped lay the groundwork for my future success but not without the occasional glitch. I remember a new Chief Financial Officer at SCF calling me into his office for a first meeting. He looked at me and said, "I have some good news and some bad news for you. Which would you like first?"

"The good news of course," I said.

"Last month you spent less money on your expense account than Morris Saffer did."

"That's great. So what's the bad news?"

"Morris put all the furniture for the new building on his credit card."

Life and work are complicated. I've paid my dues and worked long hours ever since I can remember. I know people who say you've got to work smart, not hard, and to them I say bullshit. I don't know of any successful entrepreneur who didn't work long, hard hours, especially in their early years. One of the reasons is that we're all scared shitless about failing.

I started working full-time while I was still going to university. I figure that by the time I started my own firm I had already worked a lifetime of normal work weeks. I also never missed a day of work due to illness until I was in my thirties and got food poisoning in the Cayman Islands and was hospitalized.

In fact I remember being so sick once that I couldn't drive so I had to take a limo to SCF to keep my iron man record intact. I don't think anyone else really cared; it was just anal-compulsive me being competitive even if I was just competing with myself.

Even starting my own business was the result of a competition of sorts. I was happy at SCF – with profit sharing I was making big money for a young kid and I really loved the partners and the people I worked with.

I respected Morris, Don, and David and I always said I would let them know if I was thinking about leaving. What actually transpired was wild by any measure. When I told them I might be moving on, they offered me the presidency of the Chicago office with a big piece of the action, which of course I would have to pay for through profits, or a Toronto presidency with a much smaller piece of the action.

I went to Chicago for a week to check out the operation, on the pretense of helping them with a retail pitch. Somehow while I was there the general manager of the operation, a man twenty years my elder with whom I had a fabulous relationship, figured out what I was really up to and said, "Rick, I believe you are thinking about taking over the Chicago office and I just want you to know I'd support it, my people would support it, and we would love to have it happen."

I was touched to say the least. So with this knowledge tucked in the back of my mind I headed back to Toronto only to find out that somehow the other senior VPs in Toronto had gotten wind of the situation. Jerry McDonnell was chosen to talk to me. In addition to Jerry, we had a dream team of senior VPs, including Margaret Cioffi, Julius Freilich, Terry Morgan, Donna Pearl, Anita Salis, and Isabella Carnegie. Their spokesman, Jerry, told me, "Rick, we all want you to stay and we'll support you to head up SCF here."

It wasn't meant as a coup, since Morris, Don, and David were still the partners, but it was a show of support that reflected what was already going on in the day-to-day operation.

Again I was touched to the nth degree. This was a vote of confidence by my peers, all of whom I loved and respected. Then it got really crazy, with three more opportunities coming at me boom, boom, boom. Two clients, one a developer and the other a manufacturer, both asked me if I would consider taking on a senior role – president/executive VP – in their business. In addition another major agency based in Montreal, BCP, wanted me to start a retail division for them in Toronto.

After lengthy discussions with the two clients, I let them know that although I was extremely flattered it probably was not a good fit for any of us. We agreed and stayed friends and just kept working as we had in the past with no hard feelings. These were relatively easy decisions, I must say.

In the meantime my talks with BCP were getting more and more promising. I was definitely at the "ask a friend" stage of decision-making. So I called my brother Jos and my father Frank and we all agreed to meet at my brother's place in New York for the weekend. My brother knew the business and knew the players. My father was a pragmatic and stoic numbers guy who had headed up Revenue Canada's non-resident corporate tax division before he retired.

Well, we spent a weekend listing the positives, negatives, and even the tax implications of all the options. We yapped and yapped and in the end my father thought I should stay with the tried and true at SCF. But just as Jos had pushed me out of the nest to go work for SCF, he felt that being a 50/50 owner with BCP would allow me greater personal growth. Even though he loved and respected Morris, he felt I would always be Morris's little brother if I stayed.

I was torn. I left New York without making a decision.

Over the years at SCF a number of agencies had already tried to lure me away to work for them. But none of these opportunities moved me as much as this one. BCP was founded by the legendary Jacques Bouchard and now is part of the mega agency Publicis. Yves Gougoux, the president, was the one who approached me in 1985. Yves was an enfant terrible and I really liked him, Jacques, and their company, but our budding relationship led to what became the most embarrassing business moment of my life.

The deal Yves and I were working on was for BCP to put up $1 million to start a retail ad agency based in Toronto. I would be president and 50 percent owner reporting to Yves who would be CEO of "Newco."

In the end, although it was one of the toughest decisions I ever made, I decided I didn't want to report to anyone and I was going to do my own thing. I was going to start my own agency and be my own boss.

Because Yves and I had become good friends during our negotiations I felt I owed it to him to tell him my decision in person. So I flew from Toronto to Montreal (on my dime of course) to meet him at the restaurant in the Airport Hilton.

I walked into the restaurant and was shocked to find sitting at the table not only Yves Gougoux but Jacques Bouchard and the entire senior executive of BCP waiting to welcome their new partner. Even now, more than twenty-five years later, I can't begin to express the horror I felt about this awful misunderstanding.

All I can remember saying is, "I'm not coming aboard," and Yves saying, "You're kidding" – several times.

After it became evident that I was not kidding, the room went quiet for what seemed an eternity but probably was just a few seconds.

Mercifully Jacques Bouchard finally ended the silence by saying with his tongue firmly in cheek, "This day will go down in infamy as the day the Italians screwed the French."

It was St.-Jean-Baptiste day, June 24, 1985.

As it turned out Yves, Jacques, and BCP ended up wildly successful to say the least. Yves eventually went to Paris to run Publicis Worldwide and after twenty-five years I'm still standing. So I guess the old adage "everything happens for a reason" has been proven once again.

Yves, Jacques, and the others who tried to hire me demonstrated faith in me and my talents. "If everyone else has faith in me, how come I haven't got faith in myself?" I thought. According to Rod McQueen, who featured me as one of Canada's top entrepreneurs in his book *The Last Best Hope: How to Start and Grow Your Own Business*, self-confidence is essential. "Of all the personal aspects stopping most people from launching a new business, personal confidence – the question so aptly captured by the phrase 'how come I haven't got faith in myself?' – is the first hurdle."

I realized I did have faith in myself and so on July 19, 1985, I started Padulo and Associates, later to be called Padulo Integrated, with twelve employees, zero accounts, and what I calculated to be about six months of cash flow to get some business in the door or die. I can tell you it was a scary time. I can also tell you it was a blast.

THE
LAST
BEST
HOPE

How to start and grow your own business

by the author of *The Moneyspinners* and *Risky Business*

Rod McQueen

Fanning the Fire

*"If everybody else has faith in me,
how come I haven't got faith in myself?"*

— Rick Padulo, Padulo Integrated

Rick Padulo's first job in the advertising business couldn't have been more modest. At eighteen, while still in school, he began working for his brother Joe as a research assistant – a grand label for someone who collared shoppers in Montreal to ask questions about buying habits and brand preferences. Photo shoots for clients weren't very glamorous either. There was no jetting off to Jamaica for exciting days on the beach with models, followed by pina coladas on soft evenings around the hotel pool. Instead, his first assignment was a day trip to the nearby Eastern Townships. To make matters worse, Padulo was expected to use his own Volkswagen as transportation and bring a rake to gather leaves for the photo, which would be used in a financial-services brochure.

But by the time he was twenty-three, Padulo had moved up the ladder and landed four major accounts, worth about

I

"Of all the personal aspects stopping most people from launching a new business, personal confidence – the question so aptly captured by the phrase 'how come I haven't got faith in myself?' – is the first hurdle."

With Dad and Jos.

Jos with Mummy and Daddy. Jos and I are extremely close. However, to this day we both believe we were the favourite child. How cool is that?

CHAPTER 2

WHAT'S A PADULO?

MY late father Frank Padulo was an extraordinary man. He was humble, stoic, smart, and the most principled person I've ever known. His picture should be beside the word "gentleman" in the dictionary.

Dad was a pretty black-and-white guy. On principles there were no compromises. He taught me so many things but two that stand out in my memory have helped shape my business life.

First, he said you must always "do the right thing." It may not be the easiest or most lucrative thing, or what makes you look best, but you will always know what the right thing is. You don't need to take an ethics course; you just have to do the right thing.

Second, he taught me never to give up.

"It's not how many times you get knocked down that's important it's how many times you get up," he said to me often.

These two life lessons are at the core of who we are and how we act at Padulo.

In terms of the business itself I knew from the outset that Padulo had to create a niche no one else occupied. We would be a collaborative partner focused on each client's profitability and success whether that client was a manufacturer, retailer, financial institution, or a politician looking for votes. We'd be a service company that created vertically integrated campaigns that positioned the client, provided clarity of offer/benefit, evoked emotion, and achieved excellence. The strategic thinking behind an ad would be just as important as the creative inspiration.

We weren't a retail agency, i.e., big price, small picture. Nor were we a national agency, i.e., big picture, small price. We created our own category. We said we are a transaction-based company. If you're selling something to a living, breathing human being, the branding and the selling are best done together, with the same ad budget.

Through all the changes the world has undergone since 1985, Rick's Nine Commandments remain the core of our operating philosophy. But the Nine Commandments, which I'll talk about in chapter 3, are just the framework. It's said that in the agency business your inventory goes up and down the elevator every day. Hiring the best and the brightest is the only way you make headway. My human resources policy is: "I'm looking for eagles that can fly in formation." I want people who can think for themselves but also be part of a team.

People, however, have to understand who's the lead eagle in the formation. If members of the team are diametrically opposed about something and we argue it back and forth – I can't convince you and you can't convince me – then I make the decision and whatever that decision is we get behind it

The Captain's word is Law

with enthusiasm because there's more of my money on the line than yours.

By the way, as CEO I struggle to make the best and most objective business decisions, which is not always easy. In fact I can remember being diametrically opposed to a creative strategy developed by Doug Moen, our original creative director, for our client Suzy Shier. We argued and argued in what was basically a full-on scrap and in the end I deferred my decision until the following morning.

After a sleepless night I arrived cranky and called Doug to my office. I reviewed the arguments, told him I still disagreed with his approach, and that there was more of my money on the line than his …

And then to his amazement I told him that I had decided to go with his recommendation.

In the end I based my decision on the simple fact that I trusted Doug. Given his background, expertise, and successful track record, he had a higher probability of being right on this creative issue than I did.

As it turned out the *What's Suzy Wearing?* campaign was a home run that won numerous creative awards but more importantly drove double-digit sales and profit increases for Suzy Shier, which was part of the Dylex family. Owners Irv Teitelbaum, Steve Gross, and the president Laurie Lewin were all mensches and they got it. As I like to say, our clients are the smartest people in the world. After all they hired us.

But as an aside, getting the Suzy Shier account was pretty special because of an unusual potential conflict of interest. I had done a lot of work for Dylex while at SCF, handling the Fairweather and Big Steel accounts and working for ad manager Bonnie Brooks. (Even then Bonnie was obviously destined for greater things.) The owners/partners of

Fairweather and Big Steel, Irv Levine and Lionel Robins, were awesome guys and they liked me a lot, as I did them.

Anyway, Suzy Shier (also a Dylex company) was looking for an agency and Lionel and Irv mentioned to Irv Teitelbaum (an owner of Suzy Shier) that I was out on my own and they should talk to me about their account.

So Irv tells Kathy Woods, his senior executive in Toronto, to get in touch with us.

Not being one to mince words, Kathy says to Irv, "I think you should know that your marketing manager, Kathy Melander, is sleeping with the president, Rick Padulo."

Irv says, "I don't think Padulo should get the account because of it but I also don't think he should not get the account because of it."

We were included in the review with a number of agencies but were categorically told that we had to be far better than anyone else to win. I stupidly guaranteed one of their senior executives that "we'll blow your socks off."

We were the last agency to present and at the conclusion of our presentation the executive whose socks I promised to blow off is the first client to speak. He starts out in a very somber manner and says, "You didn't blow my socks off."

I think to myself, "You idiot – when are you going to learn to keep your mouth shut?"

But then he smiles and says, "But my socks are just barely hanging onto my toenails and that's the best presentation I've ever seen."

Seems that's what the rest of the Suzy Shier executives felt too and we won the business.

Our Senior VP, Production, Isabella Carnegie, always contended that Kathy Melander (later to become Kathy Padulo) was the best client she ever had.

PLUS DE 200 BOUTIQUES DANS TOUT LE CANADA — OVER 200 STORES ACROSS CANADA

4307 VILLAGE CENTRE COURT, MISSISSAUGA, ONT. L4Z 1S2 ● TÉL.: (416) 848-6300

October 1, 1987

To Whom it May Concern,

Re: Rick Padulo

I have known Rick Padulo for three short years. In those three years, (two of which we've worked very closely together) Rick and his associates have made a very lasting impression on my company.

The calibre of work they have turned out for us time and time again, is unsurpassed anywhere else in this industry. The creativity and resources available to Ricks clients constantly amazes me. One of the main reasons for this is that Ricks high standards extend to his choice of staff at his agency. Rest assured, whoever you're dealing with at that agency, they're probably the best in their field. This was proven when our "What's Suzy Wearing" campaign was highly awarded by the Retail Council of Canada two years in a row.

If you're looking for a "yes man" to run the advertising agency you chose, then read no further. GO TO ANOTHER AGENCY! Rick Padulo will not allow you to make an error in his presence. He'll argue with you passionately when he has the facts and knows he's right. (and he usually is!!) He will never back down simply because you're the boss. Trust me, my company has learned to listen to this creative, intelligent, passionately caring man and our sales results give him a 100% track record so far.

My company has used Padulo and Associates as a full service agency for the past two years and are now signing our third year contract. We have every intention of using Rick and his associates for many years to come.

Sincerely,

Kathy Woods,
Vice President - Store Operations

KW/tm

N.B. An interesting retail factoid is that the company name DYLEX (founded by Jimmy Kay and Wilfred Posluns) was an acronym for Damn Your Lousy Excuses. Another interesting factoid is that over the years I handled Fairweather, Big Steel, Suzy Shier, L.A. Express, Thrifty's, Bluenotes, and Tip Top Tailors — when they were all dominant category leaders and basically in every shopping centre in Canada.

By the way, how we dealt with the conflict was that even though Kathy Melander was our boss, we all agreed that anything to do with financials involving the agency would go through Kathy's boss, Kathy Woods, which just made everyone's life easier.

Of course the jokes were always flying: "Kathy liked the agency so much she married the president" – or "The reason they got married is because they never had to argue about money," etc.

But the reality was that Suzy's owners were damn smart. They figured they'd get great value from the agency and then some. They figured right!

As much as I'm a maniac, I do listen, as any of my colleagues will tell you. My team is brutally honest with me. The Suzy Shier situation concerning going with Doug's creative was a great learning experience for me: Make a decision based on facts and the likelihood of success and then stick to it. What keeps you alive as an owner and CEO is that the decisions you make have to be right way more often than wrong.

As the owner of the store I sometimes begin to believe my own bullshit but I can count on my folks to remind me that there are always ways to improve and that there's no room for complacency. Our team at every level constantly surprises and delights me. I can't wait to get to the office every morning.

Recently I marched ten people into my office one after the other and put each one of them on notice – notice that they were doing a fabulous job. A morning like that is just plain good for your soul.

I also like to take three or four Paduloites out to lunch on a regular basis. Names are drawn from a hat and it's not unusual to end up with people from three different departments and seniority levels. To break the ice I borrow a self-esteem exercise from a California elementary school system in which kindergarten kids are asked, "What have you done for someone that makes you proud? What has someone done for you that make you feel good?"

I ask our folks, "What is the one thing that you have done for the company that makes you most proud? What has someone in the company done for you that makes you feel good?"

Whoever said, "All I really need to know I learned in kindergarten" was very sage. It's amazing what you learn from these questions and how it can impact the business. Years ago when interest rates were in the high teens I took a group out to lunch. One of the participants was Mary DiPietro, a shy young lady in her mid-twenties who worked in accounts receivable. When I asked her what she'd done that made her most proud she hesitated for a moment, thinking hard about her response.

Then she told us in a humble, low-key way that she had taken thirty-day receivables from 20 percent to 40 percent, thirty- to sixty-day receivables from 20 percent to 50 percent, and sixty- to ninety-day receivables from 50 percent to 10 percent.

To be honest, I may be fudging the numbers a bit because it was so long ago, but the implications of her achievement have always stuck in my mind.

In fact I remember recounting the story to our Chief Financial Officer in detail right after that lunch. He did the math and told me Mary's actions had added hundreds of thousands of dollars to our bottom line.

You know what they say: Sales are vanity, profit is sanity, and cash flow is reality!

Mary had a right to be proud; she also had a right to a promotion, raise, and bonus, which she got forthwith.

The results of Mary's pro-active actions brought about because of the pride she took in her work and the implications for all business owners are obvious. Every person in every organization is important and can impact their business to an unimaginable degree. I've never forgotten the lesson Mary taught me and I never will.

But as much as I think I'm a people person there are some people who won't work for me or with me because they think I'm a cowboy. Most of them are MBA types. We have some MBAs here so I don't hold the degree against everyone who has one but MBAs have screwed up more companies than Carter has pills. They often don't get the reality.

In the greedy 1980s and 1990s the MBA investment bankers were promoting mergers and acquisitions and financing deals. But can you think of a merger or acquisition, of the hundreds that happened, that added real value and created more jobs? The dealmakers made millions for themselves but created nothing lasting in the world of commerce. All they did was consolidate costs and cut people. The cost-slashing might have made money but it was short-sighted. You can't cost-cut your way to success.

When it comes to advertising, book-learned pragmatists usually think just about the brand. I've always said we have just one budget. We've got to build the brand and sell the product for the same money. Anything you do that doesn't achieve that goal is wrong.

Marketers go astray for other reasons too, not just because of their education. At best they deliver product awareness with some image advertising. The creative might win awards but it doesn't close the sale for the client. Ad people say they can't actualize but that's a cop-out. I take responsibility for the end sale, otherwise all I'm doing is creating a TV spot or a radio spot in a vacuum. I'm not in business to have a flashy book or win awards, though I'm proud to say that we've won more than our share of awards.

In fact I once was quoted as saying that I thought advertising awards shows were "judged by overpaid, under-talented creative hacks who were blowing smoke up each other's asses," which I guess made for a good sound bite. However, what I really meant was that the best creative is the creative that sells my client's product or service. My sole motivation is my client's success.

I led the team that created what many believe to be three of the five best retail campaigns in Canadian ad history. Everybody else in the industry combined did the other two. My top three were:

1. *Black's Is Photography*
2. *Leon's – Don't Pay a Cent Event*
3. *Because ... the Lowest Price Is the Law*, for Zellers, coupled with *I Got It Free*, for Club Z

If you ask me what I'm good at I'd say I'm a specialist in nothing but I understand a lot. I'm ordinary and by ordinary what I mean is I see things the way Joe Public sees them. I understand where people are coming from, what they're thinking, what motivates them. It's kind of intrinsic. I don't know why I know, I just know.

I have an innate ability to read people. I see the "yes" and "no" signals clearly. I can tell, be they clients or the general public, what they're thinking. You can't learn how to read people. You either have it or you don't. It's got to do with the fact that I love people. Deep down I'm a sales guy. I just want to sell my client's stuff and I want them to love me. Thank "gawd" I have a great Chief Financial / Chief Operating Officer, Kamel Mikhael or I'd be broke because I've never cared about making money for myself; I've only cared about making my clients successful and about them loving me.

How insecure is that? Can you say "entrepreneur"?

Some of the large multinational agencies that got tired of us kicking their butts in pitches actually developed specific strategies to employ against us if they knew we were involved.

The president of one such company actually called his "new biz" team into a meeting after we'd just won a pitch they were going for and asked them, "What the hell is Padulo doing to win so much?"

The consensus (as I later heard from one of the people in the room) was that we were good in general but nobody could "out retail" us in a pitch. The consensus was also that our "creative worked" and sold our clients' products and services.

Well, your honour, guilty on both counts.

Yes, we know retail better than anyone else, and yes, we do creative with sales as our primary motivator. Our focus is on selling for our client, not improving our art director's bag.

The strategy to compete against Padulo was kind of passive-aggressive. Our competitors would tell their prospect you have to worry about your brand, brand, brand and you need brand, brand, brand-building creative. Implied, if not stated, was that while we multinationals do great brand work, those other guys (Padulo) don't.

Frankly I find it flattering that competitors still employ this tactic against us. Fortunately lots of clients (then and now) just aren't buying it. But I can see the competitive concerns the rest of the ad industry had.

At the time the tactic was developed we had just won seven out of seven pitches. In fact the market was so abuzz that I got a call from Trevor Hutchings, the satirist who had been cartooning for *Marketing* magazine for decades. I was taken aback that Trevor was calling to ask if he could use me in a cartoon for the magazine. Frankly I was concerned about getting lampooned so I hesitated.

Trevor sensed my trepidation and jumped in to say, "I promise it's nothing bad."

I agreed to his request and a few weeks later the cartoon appeared. It shows two ad guys talking in a bar. One guy says to the other guy, "So far the New Year is off to a great start. I received a Christmas card on January 11 from a potential new client that simply said 'Get serious' and on the way in here I saw my bread and butter account having lunch with Rick Padulo."

"SO FAR, THE NEW YEAR IS OFF TO A GREAT START — I RECEIVED A CHRISTMAS CARD ON JANUARY 11TH FROM A POTENTIAL NEW CLIENT THAT SIMPLY SAID 'GET SERIOUS!' AND ON THE WAY IN HERE, I SAW MY BREAD AND BUTTER ACCOUNT HAVING LUNCH WITH RICK PADULO!"

Marketing Magazine

It was hysterical and to my knowledge that was the first and only time Trevor (whom I had never met) had used an actual person and company in one of his cartoons.

I got more calls from that cartoon than I got from full-page feature articles in the *Globe and Mail*. Months later I met Trevor for the first time at a lunch. I learned that in a previous life he had been the creative director of the fabled Cockfield Brown Agency and that he had been following my career with interest. He told me that he believed what we were doing was the future of the "ad biz" which was very gratifying and certainly was an ego booster. Truth is, you've got to have an ego to make it in this business because someone is always trying to whack you and you must have the strength of your personal convictions to survive – and I've been a survivor.

At that same lunch Trevor discovered that we had just gone on another winning streak and decided to do another cartoon. Well, the editorial staff at *Marketing* refused to run it. In essence they said, "Trevor, are you nuts? Everybody's going to think you're working for Padulo."

Never being one to let a good thing pass I bought space in both *Marketing* and *Strategy* and ran the cartoon as an ad, which I must say had the desired effect.

The cartoon depicts two ad guys walking down the street. One guy says to the other guy, "Stop snivelling for godsake – you were the one that said, it's in the bag – Padulo doesn't have a chance in hell."

Not only did the cartoons help to answer the "What's a Padulo?" question, they also demonstrated that the accounts we were winning and the folks we were dealing with understood who we were and what we were doing.

When we won the CIBC business it was for two reasons. First, they knew we could build their brand. Second, they

"STOP SNIVELLING FOR GODSAKE — YOU WERE THE ONE THAT SAID, IT'S IN THE BAG — PADULO DOESN'T HAVE A CHANCE IN HELL!"

Ran the above as an ad in Marketing *and* Strategy *magazines.*

knew that our retail expertise and our fanatical vertical integration at the retail brand level would help their business.

What could be more brand positioning than the slogan *Personal Vision – We're Working to See What You See* followed by *Seeing Beyond* and with the message executed through every line of communication at branch, phone, and URL levels? Up to that time no Big Five bank had ever had an agency that did everything from TV to radio to print to direct to Internet. We were even designing cards and writing their telemarketing speeches. We treated their branches like stores and it paid off for everyone.

The Padulo Group of companies, which really is the people in those companies, is unique. From me right down to a junior copywriter or media estimator everyone is empowered to do one thing and that is "the right thing." We always act in the best interest of our client. Our approach is if you must err, err on the side of the client.

So if you could distill everything down to capture the essence of "What's a Padulo?" it would simply be "doing the right thing."

Even at the very outset we did the right thing. A lot of agencies get started when employees leave and take business from their old firm with them. Not us. I didn't think it was ethical to take any business with me when I left SCF even though I "owned" the relationship with a number of SCF's larger clients. Morris, Don, and David had been good to me. We parted friends and to this day we are friends.

Holt, Renfrew & Co., Limited
ESTABLISHED 1837

50 BLOOR ST. WEST, TORONTO, ONTARIO M4W 1A1

August 1985

To Whom It May Concern:

This letter will act as verification of my long professional relationship with Rick Padulo, formerly Vice-President of Saffer, Cravit, Freedman. Richard and I have worked together over the past 10 years, since his services were first hired by Fairweather in the name of Dean Morgan Associates, Montreal. In later years, Rick was instrumental in the decision made by Dylex to turn over the Fairweather/Big Steel Man advertising business to Saffer, Cravit, Freedman, during which time I was the Advertising Manager. We thought very highly of Rick and trusted his professional skills. Rick's qualities are numerous, his marketing know-how very obvious. I wish him success in his new venture.

Bonnie Brooks-Young
Vice-President,
Sales Promotion & Marketing

Merrill Lynch

September 19, 1985

To Whom It May Concern:

I have known Richard Padulo in a professional capacity for the past five years, and have found that not only is he well respected in the industry but also offers valuable insight into the world of retailing and communication.

I would heartily recommend him to any company dealing with the cons~ at the retail level.

Yours sincerely,

Mary Jane P
Merchandisi
Investment R

MJP/cg

Mother Tucker's Food Experience

International Offices
1485 Inkster Boulevard
Winnipeg, Manitoba
R2X 1R2
Telephone (204) 633-4822

July 29, 1985

TO WHOM IT MAY CONCERN

RE: RICK PADULO

I have known Rick for just a short while and yet it seems as though we have known each other for quite some time. I think that's most simply explained by the fact that after you've met Rick, you want to get to know him. Rick's enthusiasm, his "go for it all/never say die" attitude draws you in. It's infectious. In a short time, I have seen him direct, challenge, praise, agree and disagree with his people and all in a way indicates a strong sensitivity toward them. That is how he gets the best out of them. He expects no less of anyone around him than he expects of himself.

Underneath a somewhat brash exterior, that same sensitivity extends to both clients and client markets. Although it seems at times that he comes from the hip with his comments and suggestions, Rick has proven remarkably accurate in his assessment of circumstance in our meetings.

Rick takes out into the street a solid background of experience and an immense desire to succeed. I would bet on him not just to succeed but indeed take Padulo and Associates to the leading edge of the advertising business in Canada. Padulo and Associates is a first-rate addition to Canada's advertising community.

Sincerely,

BLACK PHOTO CORPORATION LIMITED

July 23, 1985

ROBERT F. BLACK
President

TO WHOM IT MAY CONCERN

Black's and Saffers grew dramatically during the period that Rick Padulo handled Black's account. Rick has to be credited for some of this success.

The Blacks are marketing oriented and provide a great deal of the input used by Saffers in the advertising for Black's. Rick was able to take the multitude of ideas from various Black's and the Saffer people, and work to get the best of these into action.

He is patient, listens well, and explains his position well.

Rick has been a winner, and I'm sure will continue so in his own business.

Bata

August 19, 1985

To Whom It May Concern:

I have known Richard Padulo since 1982, when I came from Bata
Carribean to run the Canadian Retail Divisions of Bata and Athlete's
World.
Richard had been handling the Bata/Athlete's World advertising account
for a number of years and we spent an intense period getting to
know each other's point of view. Together we developed a strategic
direction that we felt was correct for our operation.

I believe that the strate̶ . . . . . .ics, creative input and
media implementation has

Perhaps equally importan̶
ship between Richard an̶
frank dialogue we have
effective communicatio

I know first hand tha̶
that he will continu̶

Sincerely yours,

R. ERHART
Vice President/Ge

Fairweather
Division of Dylex Limited

Mr. R. Padulo, President
Padulo & Associates
797 Don Mills Rd.
Suite 1000
Don Mills, Ontario
M3C 1V2

October 11, 1985

Dear Rick,

It has been a pleasure working with you over the past six years.
During that time, your involvement on our account at a senior level
ensured the smooth day-to-day operation of our on-going advertising
campaigns. You played a key role in helping us develop our long
term strategies - both for major media and our overall marketing
position.

Rick, one of the things that stand out about you the most in my mind
is the fact that you always stood behind and fought long and hard for
what you believed was right for us.

On behalf of Fairweather, I wish you all th̶ . . . . ur new
endeavour.

Best regar̶

Towers

July 30, 1985

William L. Atkinson
President
And Chief Executive Officer

TO WHOM IT MAY CONCERN:

Saffer Cravit & Freedman has been Towers
Department Stores' advertising agency
since 1977. In recent years, Richard
(Rick) Padulo, Senior Vice-President,
Client Services, has been the senior
account executive responsible for the
Towers account. In this capacity, he
contributed to the formulation of marketing strategy and tactics and played a
major role in the development and
implementation of advertising, sales
promotion and communications programs.

Rick enjoyed an excellent working relationship with Towers personnel at all levels -
executive, merchandise management, buying
and advertising. This was due in part to
his identification with our needs and
objectives and in part to his superior
interpersonal skills.

In my opinion, Rick Padulo has a good
understanding of retail advertising. He
is bright, enthusiastic and a man of
integrity. I would recommend him to those
seeking these attributes in a professional
relationship.

In fact Don and David both worked at Padulo for a number of years.

When I started all I had was a series of letters of recommendations from happy clients and even the retail analyst of Merrill Lynch. One such letter came from Bonnie Brooks (now president of the Bay) who in 1985 was VP of Holt Renfrew. I had dinner with Bonnie recently and reminisced with her about her role in getting me started. It was fun to be able to thank her again in person.

Shortly after I got started Morris actually asked me to take a few tiny pieces of business that cost his large machine more money to handle than the income he could earn. I was delighted to do so. My little company could eke out a small profit on this work because our overheads were so low.

Morris also did two other things for which I am eternally grateful.

As a friend he fronted me some money, collateralized by Padulo shares, which I paid back quickly and with interest. Morris and I were such good friends that for years a lot of people thought he was a silent partner in my company but he wasn't. However, Morris's money, my own money, and a bank line of credit combined to get me going.

The other thing he did was give me my office furniture, which has great sentimental value because it was Morris's first big-time "office set." The beautiful travertine marble desk, credenza, and tables remain my office furniture to this day. When I offered to buy the furniture from Morris, he said, "Kid, take it. You've earned it and I hope it's as lucky for you as it was for me."

Morris always had a big, big heart. He still gives me inspiration because I just wouldn't want to let my friend and mentor down.

THANK YOU MORRIS SAFFER!

CHAPTER 3

RICK'S NINE COMMANDMENTS

THE day I started my own company my father Frank called me and said, "How do you like your first day of unemployment?"

The realization that from that moment I had to kill what I ate was at once exhilarating and terrifying – however, it did breed commitment.

I've always been characterized as a street-fighting entrepreneur and that's probably why I love retail so much. I've worked for the first, second, or third largest retailer in just about every category in both Canada and the United States. In my career I've won and worked with clients who had advertising budgets totalling in the billions of dollars.

I've never been accused of being overly diplomatic so I'll unabashedly say that my clients always do better with me than without me. And as Dizzy Dean once said, "It ain't bragging if you can do it!"

I'm often asked what the elements are that made Padulo – the company – so successful and I think I've figured it out although I must say that I've also found that once you get there, there isn't there anymore. Every time I think I've got the retail game figured out something sneaks up and bites me in the ass. I also believe that the things that made our company successful are the same things that made our clients successful and it's not "rocket science" – it's Rick's Nine Commandments.

RICK'S NINE COMMANDMENTS

I   THOU SHALT BE TRANSACTION BASED

II   THOU SHALT BE CUSTOMER FOCUSED

III   THOU SHALT BE NON-COMPETITIVE

IV   THOU SHALT THINK CHANGE QUOTIENT

V   THOU SHALT MAKE THE USUAL UNUSUAL
      AND THE UNUSUAL USUAL

VI   THOU SHALT BE FANATICALLY VERTICALLY
      INTEGRATED AND MAINTAIN CONTINUITY

VII   THOU SHALT HAVE A SENSE OF URGENCY,
      A PASSION FOR EXCELLENCE AND A HEALTHY
      DISRESPECT FOR THE WAY THINGS ARE

VIII   THOU SHALT REMEMBER THE STORE IS THE BRAND

IX   THOU SHALT UNDERSTAND THE IMPORTANCE
      OF LEADERSHIP/CULTURE/SERVICE

DIRECT&PERSONAL

by Billy Sharma

Rick Padulo

A true survivor in the jungle called Advertising.

I don't consider myself a direct marketing specialist; I am a marketing specialist with an intimate understanding of direct mail. My roots are in retail and I learned very early on that relational marketing and the life-long value of a customer was very important.

One of the things that Rick Padulo told me when we met was, "There are two pieces of advice my father gave me which have guided me in life and in business: it's not how many times you get knocked down, it's how many times you get up, and always do the right thing, you'll know what it is. It may not be the easiest, the most lucrative or what makes you look the best, but you will always know what the right thing is."

Rick is not only a true survivor, having experienced many highs and lows in his life, but a street-fighter when it comes to this jungle called advertising. Yet he has never been a dirty fighter. All the successes that he and his agency have achieved are hard fought and won on merit and chutzpah.

As he said with excitement: "I love the biz. I love working every piece of it. I like knowing what's going on in intimate detail. However, if you asked other people I guess I might be characterized as a hunter and a survivor. I love the chasing of new biz. I love being involved in developing a new program that will affect our client's business in a positive way.

"With my roots being in retail I learned very early on that relational marketing and the life-long value of a customer was very important.

"Direct marketing is so retail friendly. What a joy and relatively easy sale it is when you can say to a retailer: you spend this, you get this back and you can measure your revenue and profit to the penny.

"However, our key strength and our success exist in the fact that we are marketing specialists. There is no glaring separation between the direct marketing team and the advertising team. Silos are not allowed to exist, the team is the team and there is one profit centre. There is no silo or vested interest of one group over another and that synergy is why we are

"As corny as it may sound our 'meme' — our DNA — is that we want our client/partners, our vendor/partners and our own folks to say we love these people, this place and this attitude.

"Sure, it's a very lofty goal and obviously we can't lose sight of reality because we're far from perfect. But I can tell you in all honesty that we are committed to the

"Whether it is a pair of socks, a brand of car or getting someone to vote for a politician, eventually you have to sell 'product, service or a brand' to a living breathing person.

"I believed from the beginning that the marketing process had to be integrated and in fact we were the first marketing company to include the word 'integrated' in our name.

"Over the years our company has done integrated direct marketing programs for many categories including credit cards, casinos, cars, energy, insurance and telecommunications."

Rick Padulo was born and raised in Montreal.

"When I was 16 years old I worked part time as a research assistant while going to school. I first went to Algonquin College in Ottawa then Concordia in Montreal. I studied the science of technology and leisure in a course called Recreology at Algonquin and then I studied marketing, analytics and economics at Concordia.

"I stood around in the Westmont Shopping Centre handing out questionnaires and then did a report on

1. THOU SHALT BE TRANSACTION BASED

When we refer to a transaction there is an intrinsic understanding that helps define how we think. We believe that a transaction is a cyclical, living organism that feeds itself. We believe that the last second of one transaction is the first second of the next transaction.

Long before the marketing world was touting CRM (Customer Relationship Marketing) and DM (Direct Marketing), and overusing terms like database analytics, cloning, and the lifetime value of a client, I was talking transaction-based advertising. In retail it was "blocking and tackling" in its simplest form.

I delivered marketing speeches all over the world about the importance of the cyclical nature of a transaction because research suggested that if you made a customer happy they might tell three people but if you pissed them off they'd tell ten people. So I always pointed out that in retail you had to be 300 percent better just to stay even.

Boy have things changed! In today's climate of social networking, if you piss someone off (especially a female someone) they will tell twenty-nine people in seconds – which means you have to be 3000 percent better. That's a tiny factoid that should keep most retailers up at night.

MAPPING OUR MEME

meme /mi:m/ n.Biol. an element of a culture or system of behaviour that is passed from one individual to another by non-genetic means, esp. imitation.

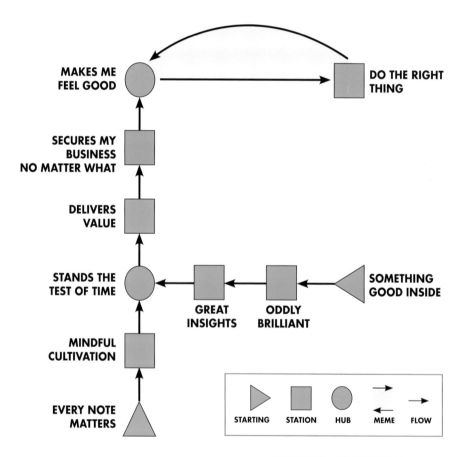

MAKES ME FEEL GOOD

DO THE RIGHT THING

SECURES MY BUSINESS NO MATTER WHAT

DELIVERS VALUE

STANDS THE TEST OF TIME

GREAT INSIGHTS

ODDLY BRILLIANT

SOMETHING GOOD INSIDE

MINDFUL CULTIVATION

EVERY NOTE MATTERS

STARTING · STATION · HUB · MEME · FLOW

SCIENTIFIC INTELLIGENCE

2. THOU SHALT BE CUSTOMER FOCUSED

When I first started Padulo we used to say we were customer driven but we soon changed the word "driven" to "focused" and here's why. We all agreed that our customers were of paramount importance. However after hours of debate we also agreed that the word "driven" meant we were reacting and just doing our clients' bidding rather than doing the right thing or at least counselling our client/partner to do the right thing even if we took heat for doing so. Yes we wanted to surprise and delight our clients but it was more than that.

In fact in our most recent agency self-diagnostic we worked with a company called Scientific Intelligence, which reaffirmed our position. They have an incredible process by which they map your MEME, which is really the DNA of your organization. What we realized was that we all want our clients to LOVE US. What we also realized was that we were always focused on doing the right thing. Interestingly, when you get down to the short strokes, "to love" there has to be a mutual respect and an understanding that the parties will always aim to "do the right thing" for each other.

3. THOU SHALT BE NON-COMPETITIVE

In our vernacular being non-competitive means doing things in ways that nobody else is doing. Our thinking is basically that if you're merely competitive and you do a "slam dunk" you're just going to be equal to the next competitor.

CANADA'S WEEKLY BUSINESS AND FINANCIAL NEWSPAPER

FINANCIAL **TIMES**

FINANCIAL TIMES OF CANADA ■ APRIL 10-16, 1993

Padulo: A David among the Goliaths

Padulo's secret, though, is not just offering his clients a full range of services. In the 1980s, after all, "full service" became the industry buzzword as agencies scrambled to create and buy up PR agencies, direct mail and telemarketing operations, promotions houses, almost anything they could get their hands on, and often at top dollar. But costs often grew just as quickly, and sometimes faster. When the boom times ended, agency behemoths like the U.K.-based WPP Group — owners of two multinational agency giants, J. Walter Thompson Company and Ogilvy and Mather — and Saatchi and Saatchi were revealed to have brought very little value to their clients through all their financial machinations.

Padulo, in contrast, has managed to develop a full range of services without the hierarchy, bureaucracy and payroll fat.

Agency CFO Rootenberg attributes much of the Padulo success to an "extremely flat" management structure. On the account management side, there are just three tiers of management — an account executive and account supervisor, re-

two or three more tiers. And, says Joe Padulo, in instances "where the confidence level" is high, the agency has creative people meet with clients alone rather than follow the age-old industry habit of having an account person go along even if all they do is open doors. Most agencies are trying to do similar things. But many can't make the change.

"There's a lot of fine companies out there with a lot of great intellectual capital," says Rick Padulo. "But culturally and operationally they're dinosaurs. I love the position we're in, being the David among the Goliaths, with our ability to move and do things without having to answer to London or New York or wherever."

Padulo's learned a lot about running his own business from clients like Zellers, who he says have been able to offer lower prices to consumers and keep, and even grow, profit margins by ratcheting down costs. "We are measuring every one of our cost factors against industry statistics, and our mandate is to be way above the average in terms of productivity," he explains.

Padulo likes to say he's perfected a hybrid marketing organization

Being non-competitive means you're doing something special. When you're doing stuff nobody else is doing – in essence being non-competitive – you stand out in a positive way. The joy of it is that it's about clear-headed thinking, not spending your client's money.

My favourite, favourite, favourite thing to do is to work closely and transparently with a client because I can always get them so much more for their money than anyone else. Just recently we did a media buy for a client where for $1.3 million* (gross) we got them $3.8 million (gross) of rate card value in radio, out-of-home, and print. The real dollar savings for the client will pay our fees for years.

In media terms when we speak of "gross" it means we're receiving commissions from the media. This means we made the commission that paid for our services and still got almost 300 percent of the rate card value for our client. By the way this real-life media scenario, which took place in Q4 of 2010, is a classic example of being non-competitive not only from our point of view as the agency but also from our client's point of view.

Our client gave us total freedom in buying, negotiating, and selecting media. As a result our client far surpassed awareness objectives and – best of all – dramatically increased planned sales. When you have a client that doubles sales and gets an almost 300 per cent increase in exposure with a zero out-of-pocket expense, you very likely have a supremely happy client.

*In the ad business, agencies receive a 15 percent commission from the media. So we would buy $100 worth of media for $85.

54

4. THOU SHALT THINK CHANGE QUOTIENT

We value CQ (change quotient) as highly as we do IQ (intelligence quotient). In fact it would be impossible to work within our family of companies without being able to embrace change. Today no company can succeed without this fundamental component in their philosophy.

We look for people who embrace change rather than fight it, all the while recognizing that this is not an easy road to follow. So many things are changing so quickly we all can feel overwhelmed.

There's a story I like to tell that goes like this: Two guys are going down to the river to fish and as they come around a bend they see a huge grizzly bear rearing up on its hind legs and growling. Suddenly the bear comes down on all fours and starts chasing them. The fishermen start running and praying faster than atheists in an earthquake. The guy behind is screaming, "We're never going to outrun this bear." The guy in front says, "All I have to do is outrun you!"

Therein lies the moral of my story: Never give up trying to be number one. You can't be ahead on everything all the time, and you can't know everything all the time, but you can know more and do more than your competitor. If you focus on that and you've got guts then you'll do just fine. Set a target and always try to surpass it.

There is no longer any such thing as conventional wisdom. You must always be looking for an edge and more often than not that edge involves some form of change.

'THE LOWEST PRICE IS THE LAW'

'DON'T PAY A CENT EVENT'

'BLACK'S IS PHOTOGRAPHY'

5. THOU SHALT MAKE THE USUAL UNUSUAL AND THE UNUSUAL USUAL

Both creatively and strategically you have to make the unusual usual. You must be able to take a complicated message such as a payment plan with lots of legal "mice type" that makes it unusual to the consumer and make it usual for them "strategically" as in "Don't pay principal, interest, or tax for a year." Or, even better, more simply and creatively as in "Don't Pay a Cent Event."

The secret is to help a client take a usual message like "We have low prices" and strategically make it understandable to everyone – including their own people – that we will have the lowest opening price point in every product category on our flyer cover. But to do so creatively, not by using a "me too" statement like "We promise low prices" or "We guarantee low prices." You make it unusual by saying *Because … the Lowest Price Is the Law.*

Any agency is supposed to be competent in all of the marketing disciplines. That's usual. But if you consider yourself a high-end service company that just happens to be great in advertising and marketing, now that's unusual.

There is always a way to make the usual unusual and the unusual usual. My friends and clients kid the hell out of me because years ago Sarah Hampson wrote an article in *Toronto Life* describing me as "The Rick." The article won an award as the best business article in Canada and I guess it was well read because everyone started calling me that. However, it wasn't like "The Donald." Instead, The Rick name revolved around the concept of usual and unusual.

As with every agency we always have internal strategic/ creative presentations before we meet the client. At our internal presentations everyone tried "knocking me on my ass" with something extraordinary. The process came to be known as Beat the Rick.

The internal presentations became like a game show: You won if you beat The Rick. The thinking was that I'd been involved in so many presentations for so many clients that I'd seen and done everything – well, almost everything. If my folks could excite, surprise, and delight me – by making the usual unusual or the unusual usual – then we would for sure score with the client because they had Beat the Rick.

TORONTO LIFE

one-button, two-button or three-button. She was referring to the buttons on her blouse. How creative. And then there is Ian Mirlin, a dishevelled writer revered in the business not only for his work (Kodak, Levi's and Evian) but also for

a Tip Top customer in a Tip Top suit, fidence; a couple waltzing on a Simn satisfied customers.

Into the white space pops Padulo, big smile. Th suit with h slick, cut to bald vanity s hint of self- comes off ir courting app see his treeh

"I've seen everything, so if an idea can beat The Rick, then a client is going to go uh-huh and buy it"

his ability to silence a room of pontificating suits with a single whispered observation. True guru.

And now, Padulo. He calls internal creative reviews "Beat The Rick" sessions: "a game, a contest, because I've seen everything, you know, so if an idea can beat The Rick, then a client is going to go uh-huh and buy it." His success suggests that he may be what he says he is—namely, the future of advertising. Forty-four years old and in just over ten years he

"Wanna tour?" Warm and friendl shoulder assumption of intimacy. H doors painted with trompe l'oeil sce "These are the cans. I paid OCA [On dents $300 a door to paint them. Fu the halls. Pokes his head into office hospital emergency ward. He utters " anyone is there. Responds "Cool, co

BEAT THE RICK IS A GAME LIKE BEAT THE CLOCK

TORONTO LIFE

DECEMBER 1995 $3.25

PADULO COMPANIES

The adma

His upstart agency is called Padulo Integrated, but the sign on top of the building just says PADULO. The Rick, as he calls himself, is too busy winning to be modest *By Sarah Hampson*

who ate Toronto

YONGE AND ST. CLAIR IS A VERY STRAIGHT INTERSECTION. Okay, there's Joe Di Maggio's Wet Paint Café, a restaurant where artists come to paint at night. Cool. But that's an exception. Sam The Record Man has a small store. Such restraint. The Badminton and Racquet Club politely self-effaces behind buildings on the southwest corner. Snore. Remember: it was only last year that Ira Berg, contributor to Rosedale Wife snootydom, stocked clothes by designer Betsey Johnson. Shiny, short, stretchy stuff.

When Rick Padulo moved his advertising agency here in 1993 from Bayview Avenue, he erected a poster in a local bus shelter that read, STARTING SEPTEMBER 27TH, YONGE AND ST. CLAIR BECOMES YONGE AND PADULO.... THERE GOES THE NEIGHBOURHOOD. For him, it was an arrival. For everyone else, a departure. On top of the office block (named the Padulo Building) appears the name PADULO in fat, green letters. No elegant corporate acronym. It wouldn't belong. You'll see why.

Well, your timing couldn't be better," nattered Padulo when I called him last year to suggest a story on his company. "This is shaping up to be the biggest single day in the history of Canadian advertising. We pitched a piece of business today that if we get it will be the biggest single coup in years."

"What is it?"

"Can't tell. Confidential. I'm on a high. This is a great day. It's been with the same agency for a hundred years—that's what the agency says, the client says less. [The official number is eighty-two.] It's big. I mean really big. Huge [pronounced *oouge*]. We

figured out a way to add billions of dollars in revenue to their business over the next five years. Lookit—if the other agency wins it, I don't really care. Well, I care. But we were hot. We did the best job ever."

"Who's the other agency?"

"McKim. They're the largest advertising agency in Canada. We were hot, though. It's CIBC."

"CIBC? The whole account?"

"The works."

"When will you know you got it?"

"Soon, I think. But there were lots of buy-signals."

"Buy-what?"

"Buy-signals."

"Uh-huh."

And he won it. Without even a formal review—the traditional industry practice of putting an account up for grabs to a number of agencies. The Canadian Imperial Bank of Commerce invited only Padulo Integrated and McKim Baker Lovick/BBDO, now simply BBDO, to the "closed pitch." Worth an estimated forty million dollars annually, the entire account fell to Padulo Integrated, which had handled the bank's direct-response business for three years and shown an interest in the rest. It *was* a big day in Canadian advertising, a win, as Padulo would say, "that changed the perception of us on the street from hot young turks to hot, but a player." Megawatt grin.

Not that unusual things don't happen in the advertising business. They do. People argue about the viscosity of sinus cavities before and after a dose of decongestant; spend hours talking about how to shake a box of Glosettes; debate the charac-

The Rick is into New Age. Change. Interactive. The Padulo Institute for Tomorrow. Is hot, hot, hot

FANATICALLY VERTICALLY INTEGRATED

6. THOU SHALT BE FANATICALLY VERTICALLY INTEGRATED AND MAINTAIN CONTINUITY

Padulo Integrated Inc. was the first agency to put the word "Integrated" in its name. We are fanatical about the bottom-up, top-down integration of messaging in all our campaigns.

We are fanatical about the umbrella strategy being reflected at every touch point. One of the reasons we've always whacked the competition is that once we arrive at a strategy and a creative positioning we stick with it. We don't run around like chickens with our heads cut off when new management comes in on the client side or we put a new creative team on the account on the agency side.

If a positioning based on sound strategy was in place there had to be a hell of a good reason to change it and a creative team's desire to "do something new" was definitely not a good reason.

The whole is always greater than the sum of the parts. You can freshen the execution or employ new media but never change for the sake of change and give up the enormous equity that has been built, often with millions of media dollars behind it. It seems like such a simple concept but it's one of the major reasons we preempted the competition over and over again. Clients and agencies always get tired of something long before the general public does. If a strategic/creative position is founded in strength, don't mess with it.

Three of the positioning campaigns in this book became storefront signs:

Zellers – Because ... the Lowest Price Is the Law
Rexall – A Pharmacy First
Black's Is Photography

(Although in the case of many of the Black's stores, mall landlords would not allow the slogan as part of the sign so the stores stuck it on permanent signs in their stores that were very visible to passersby.)

7. THOU SHALT HAVE A SENSE OF URGENCY, A PASSION FOR EXCELLENCE AND A HEALTHY DISRESPECT FOR THE WAY THINGS ARE

I am not a patient man. I have found that any successful client I've ever had is not patient. The more nimble – the more profitable. I believe that in any business at any level there must be a sense of urgency. I can't stand lazy or laissez-faire. If you don't have a sense of urgency you are not working in my family of companies!

It used to be that business operated on the premise "speed, quality, and efficient cost – pick any two." Those days are gone forever. Today you've got to be fast, deliver quality, and be cost efficient.

In order to do all that you must have a healthy disrespect for the way things are. There is just no such thing as conventional wisdom anymore.

WHATCHA GONNA DO?

The only wrong way to do the T.O. Toss is to not do it at all. There are trash cans and recycling bins
all over the city for you to use, so do the T.O. Toss and help keep our city clean!

*T.O. TOSS was a pro bono job we did for Mel Lastman and the City of Toronto,
a campaign to toss your garbage and keep the city clean. My buddy Mike
Bullard generously donated his time to be part of the campaign.*

CANADA'S WEEKLY BUSINESS AND FINANCIAL NEWSPAPER

FINANCIAL TIMES

FINANCIAL TIMES OF CANADA ■ APRIL 10-16, 1993

▶ INSIDE STORY

Full service

Lots of agencies talk about it, but Richard Padulo's Toronto-based Padulo Advertising Inc. is showing the industry how to be a comprehensive marketing consultant, grow dramatically and prosper

PAGE 14

FULL SERVICE

Lots of agencies talk about it, but Toronto-based Padulo Advertising Inc. is showing the industry how to be a comprehensive marketing consultant, grow dramatically and prosper

AS USUAL, Richard Padulo is racing around his midtown Toronto agency, Padulo Advertising Inc., doing at least 10 things at once. First of all, he's explaining why his shop is on such a hot streak — seven for seven in new business pitches, including Black's Photography and the Ontario Honda Dealers Association — for more than $20-million, a hefty increase of nearly 50% in added billings since January. This, while the rest of the advertising industry is still largely wrapped in recession.

But Padulo is also showing off his personal collection of dark abstract paintings by Croatian-Canadian artist Nikola Nikola, and taking a quick phone call from an old friend, laid off and looking for career advice. The agency chief is, of course, also giving a grand tour of

In the dimmed board room, dominated by a huge mahogany table, two TVs and a giant projection screen, Padulo and agency vice-president Bill MacDonald preview the Nutri/System presentation. The agency's conducted nine hours of focus groups, developed a new positioning line ("The science of weight loss, and feeling good") and even whipped up some new packaging. They've pulled together a so-called "ripomatic" TV spot — a speculative commercial that uses footage from other spots to give the idea of what the finished product will look like — complete with new jingle. The kicker: a personal endorsement from Padulo's older brother, Joe, an agency VP who signed up for the Nutri/System program and lost eight pounds in barely three weeks.

"Anybody that beats us," Padulo says after wowing the Nutri/System people, "deserves to win it, because we were hot."

Hot he is, but the agency's strength lies in diversity rather than excellence in any one area. Padulo, for instance, is not especially known for blazing creative work. Many of its campaigns are ex-

That catapults Padulo into the ranks of the country's 20 biggest agencies, and among the largest half-dozen or so of the shrinking ranks of those that remain entirely Canadian-owned.

Not that Padulo has gone untouched by the recession. Its cash flow was strained last year when two clients were unable to pay bills totalling more than $800,000. One, Pascal Furniture, has since gone out of business. The other — who Padulo declines to name — may yet make good on its debts. But in the meantime, Padulo carried their obligations, mostly to Toronto-region radio stations, and eventually paid all creditors 100 cents on the dollar.

As a result, there were no salary increases in 1992. On the other hand, no one was let go, either — a boast few agencies can make. With the new account wins, 1993 will see "a major profit," Padulo says, adding: "Next year, it'll be big money. Big money."

That's a contrast to the industry, generally. The old rules of the game have evaporated, and old-line, full-service integrated ad agencies have responded sluggishly. Even as the recession is said to be ending, cli-

8. THOU SHALT REMEMBER THE STORE IS THE BRAND

I've always operated on the premise that the Store is the Brand. I believe that every piece of communication must position the client but also sell. You've got to brand and sell with the same budget. Sales overnight; brands over time.

Every piece of communication must:

a) Position the brand

b) Have clarity of offer

c) Evoke an emotion

d) Be excellent

Your brand is like the air you breathe: It is all around and is part of everything you do and say. Retail is detail and every detail makes up your brand essence. In retail you must always sweat the small stuff.

LEADERSHIP
A RALLYING CRY THAT
RESONATES

9. THOU SHALT UNDERSTAND THE IMPORTANCE OF PEOPLE/ LEADERSHIP/CULTURE/SERVICE

Our clients are the smartest people in the world … after all they hired us! An idea, a concept, a strategy, a tactic, a creative execution – all of these have to be socialized and be universally understood and accepted to maximize success.

Which requires inspired leadership, vision, and brand ambassadors. The best clients truly do get the best work because they are an integral part of everything that happens. When everyone is pulling together there is traction.

It is never easy to achieve great goals. It is frickin' hard work and its always complicated. Inspired leadership is always the difference. Vision, focus, decisiveness, responsibility, and staying the course are not just the cost of entry but the path to success. It's all about engagement of the people (the head) and belief in the plan (the heart).

Obama's *Yes We Can* message or Mike Harris's *Common Sense Revolution* are what separates the true leaders from the wannabes. Like them or not, these politicians had a rallying cry that resonated. Every winner has.

And there is one other key observation that I've made working with some very extraordinary leaders and to me it's the most important characteristic: When the chips are really, really, really down, the absolute worst they can be, that's when the extraordinary leaders back off trying to squeeze the crap out of their people. Great leaders circle the wagons, get their people engaged in a plan, and execute the strategy together. Most often the greater the adversity the greater the upside – including the additional benefit of team building. Nothing makes a team better than digging out of the crap together.

I know this because I've had the privilege of seeing many extraordinary leaders at work.

I know this because in every instance when my own organization has been severely challenged we not only have survived but also have come out of it better than before.

So there you have it … go be successful … just kidding! There's more to it than that. I've only just begun.

Read on!

THE GREATER THE UPSIDE

THE GREATER THE ADVERSITY

TORONTO LIFE

The meeting is an example, Padulo says, of what happens when he's asked to handle an account, even though in this case he's simply giving Petty advice as a favour. The Padulo team fights over a piece of business, he says. To see who can come up with the best idea.

"You have a cat? Anyone have a cat?" Petty addresses the

Padulo invented Leon's "Don't Pay a Cent Event." "He's not from this planet," says Leon's wife

ring of Padulos at the start of the meeting. Some nods. "Names?"

"George," barks one.

"Tristan," mumbles another.

"Ernie," comes a third.

Petty adopts an infomercial tone. "Imagine Ernie does a do-

Hi-ya, Sa-rah, ba-by!" Padulo maining questions. The Rick cord: you see him immediately

He says things are nuts, the w ity is where it's at, business is b

how's li
the first
last nigl
4:30 in
often do

"Sma
back w
college,

was real aggressive. I used to
It was kinda a joke. But the o
was catch the ball. There would
ing. All I would see was the b
brother and business partner, o
ambition from wanting more th

CHAPTER 4

LEON'S – DON'T PAY A CENT EVENT

I N the late 1970s I rented a very cool two-storey penthouse apartment in Toronto. It was fall and I planned to have family and friends come over for Christmas. I wanted to be proud of my new place. I needed furniture for the den and a bedroom set in the guest room but I was a kid with no cash.

I was working for the advertising firm Saffer Cravit & Freedman and had just been to a meeting at Leon's Furniture. They told me they didn't spend much money advertising furniture in November or December because everybody was thinking about buying Christmas presents. As a result those two months were traditionally slow for furniture sales. Based on what was going on in my own life, plus the fact that I wanted to get Leon's to do some ad spending, I thought wouldn't it be great if I could buy furniture now, get my place ready for Christmas, and still have presents under the tree because l didn't have to pay for the furniture until much later?

Because there was very little brand awareness in furniture the only way anything got sold was on deep discounts, 30-40-50 percent off, which everyone was doing and not making much money in the process. For furniture sales my idea was a marketer's dream. What if we asked for a small down payment and deferred the rest of the payments, interest free?

I had studied the company so I understood its fixed and variable costs, margin structure, return on investment, risk management, and "price off" implications. I did the math and thought, "If they do this it'll cost them way less to carry the money than if they took deep markdowns."

We did our homework, we understood the business, so the strategy was no accident. Once the strategy made sense in financial terms it became a matter of figuring out how to creatively "market the markdowns."

Right from when Ablan Leon started the company in 1909 Leon's offered some kind of credit. But for me advertising has always been about trying to make the usual unusual and the unusual usual. So although some form of a credit plan was usual what we were proposing for Leon's was unusual.

"Mr. Tom" Leon and the rest of the family had the vision to buy into the concept and the rest is history. Leon's blew the doors off in sales in a time period when they traditionally just tread water. Almost three decades later the concept of the *Don't Pay a Cent Event* remains a cornerstone of the Leon's marketing strategy, one that almost everyone in the industry has emulated.

In retrospect it was my personal situation coupled with my connectivity with people and markets that propelled me to come up with the *Don't Pay a Cent Event* concept for Leon's. But I didn't just stop there and this is another difference between most ad people and me. Working with clients is more than marketing and advertising. I took the idea and the campaign to the next level by spending time in the stores and talking to the owners to learn all I could about the Leon family business.

From one store in Welland, Ontario, Leon's expanded across the country. The late and great Mr. Tom, as he was affectionately known throughout the furniture industry, was a second-generation leader, and Leon's is now run by the third generation, Mr. Tom's son, Terry Leon. Unlike some family businesses that make the mistake of giving a job to anyone from the gene pool, at Leon's you get a job only if you earn it.

The fact is that my personal circumstances that Christmas and what was happening in the market (money was tight) led to the genesis of the idea that revolutionized the furniture business with a unique deferred payment plan. What nobody, including me, realized was just how powerful a primary motivator the *Don't Pay a Cent Event* would become. It not only revolutionized furniture store marketing in Canada but it also got picked up in the United States and eventually became a worldwide strategy for the retail furniture industry.

When we launched the event at Leon's sales went through the roof but in every meeting I had with the Leon family I insisted that we keep our mouths shut about the program's success. We didn't want anyone to copy our idea.

This was certainly not typical for me since I have always found it hard to stay mum but it was in my client's best interest and that was that. It was amazing how well the Leon's family kept the secret for so long. I should not have been surprised because the whole family was low key and humble. It was so in keeping with their character to put on a sad face and say we're getting by in answer to the constant questions, "How are sales? How's the *Don't Pay a Cent Event* working for you?"

It wasn't too long – toward the mid-1980s – before we heard that The Brick was coming to Toronto. Mark Leon was running the west for Leon's and it was a sales war in that region with Leon's and The Brick going toe-to-toe. The Brick was so disciplined and its owners, the Comrie brothers – John, Fred, and Bill – knew how to manufacture sales. There's no other way to put it. They were hurting Leon's sales in the west, so the news that they were coming onto our home turf got everyone's attention. I did some back-channel research and learned that The Brick was going to spend aggressively on the launch with a budget of $7 to $10 million, which was big money in those days. The Leons were my family. This assault on their business was an assault on my business and it was keeping me up at night.

To offset the Brick attack we tackled them at the level of their strength. When we first launched the *Don't Pay a Cent Event* it did not include appliances. According to conventional wisdom there wasn't enough margin in appliances to offer big discounts, let alone credit deals.

I convinced Leon's to include appliances and we advertised like hell in the months leading up to The Brick's launch. As a result we took a ton of appliance sales out of the market just before The Brick opened. We preempted their strength and they opened with nothing like the sales they were looking for. For them it was like getting whacked on their first poker hand of the night. When your "full with aces over" gets beat by a "straight flush" you play a little scared for a while.

Mr. Tom and I talked about the "coup" many times over the years and we were convinced that the ramifications of The Brick's false start greatly retarded their growth and impact in Ontario. The Brick was a few years getting on track but they were and remain too good to go away. Even to this day it's a pitched battle with The Brick manufacturing sales with GWPs (gifts with purchase), Bogos (buy one get one free), big price-off promotions, and some deferred payment and Leon's selling deferred payment with some price-off promotions.

The Brick runs their version of the *Don't Pay a Cent Event* but they don't lead with it. I worked for The Brick in later years and they never really acknowledged its power. It just wasn't part of The Brick's DNA. Frankly there are many variables that make certain promotional concepts work for some retailers; one size definitely does not fit all.

The concept worked so well for Leon's because they had more money than you know who.

It's interesting, however, that eventually other retail categories started to employ the strategy with the first aggressive go-to-market launch being in the automotive industry. But what a dumb, dumb mistake it was for them. The marketing people committed marketing malpractice: the variables were too different.

First of all, automobiles have brands; you buy brands. When it comes to furniture nobody (certainly at the mass market level) is looking for a Cadillac sofa or a Chrysler bedroom set.

Second, not only did the strategy undermine automotive brands, the industry as a whole didn't have the margins that the furniture industry had to play with. Most of the car companies jumped on it as soon as the first one launched and they all cost themselves profits. It was probably one of the worst marketing moves in the history of advertising.

Of course there were many other reasons beyond the *Don't Pay a Cent Event* that brought about the success of Leon's. The company owns a lot of its real estate, has little debt, and operates frugally. The late Marge Leon was not a certified accountant but she was Chief Financial Officer. I remember Tom telling me one time that Marge had put a note in her book saying, "Tom Leon took home three rolls of toilet paper." She told him he had to replace that toilet paper and by golly he did.

Mr. Tom was an "aw shucks" kind of a guy, acting like he was from the country, always giggling and joking. Because he didn't come across as an intellectual, people often under-estimated him but he was smart – and he was smart enough to realize who was smart around him.

I always kidded Mr. Tom that he and his family reminded me of Lebanese horse traders. They were so tight they squeaked, but if they said they were going to do something they did it. If they shook your hand you could take it to the bank. They always wanted to make money. Oh and by the way they wanted you to make money too but not so much!

Our current creative director at Padulo, Chris Stavenjord, who early in his career did a stint working at Leon's as their in-house creative director, told me a story which I have to share, one that had to do with Mr. Tom's older brother, Mr. Louis, who was CEO before Mr. Tom. As Chris tells it:

My first meeting with an outside supplier was also the first time I was introduced to Mr. Louis, then chairman of the board of Leon's Furniture. After writing and directing their commercials for years I was transferred from Calgary a few weeks prior and had booked a meeting in the executive boardroom with a Toronto production house to discuss our immediate needs.

As I entered the boardroom I discovered Mr. Louis sound asleep on one of the couches. I stopped and pondered: Do I wake the chairman and continue with the meeting, or maybe seek a second opinion? Thankfully I chose the latter option and walked into Mark Leon's office, today's current chairman, and in a respectful tone uttered, "Ummm, Mark, uhh, I have a meeting in five minutes and your dad's asleep in the boardroom."

I have so much respect for the entire Leon family and it can be crystallized in the manner that Mark handled it as he promptly gave his father's toes a shake and said, "DAD GET UP and get the hell out. Chris needs the room now."

That afternoon Mr. Louis dropped by my office and in a very disarming way introduced himself and with a chuckle apologized for the incident and then asked how the meeting went. I of course said terrific and when pressed further admitted it was actually my first meeting with that company.

He went silent for a second and then said, "Son, when I meet a company for the first time I always say … Look, I know you're going to screw me, so take as much as you want – all I ask is you leave a little bit for me."

I laughed, smiled, and said, "Mr. Louis, I will remember that."

When I started working with Leon's, Canada was mired in a recession. One of the first things I did was visit the presidents of all their major suppliers. Many clients would be afraid for me to do that. Mr. Tom wasn't afraid. He was secure in his own skin.

I was an advocate and an ambassador while gleaning information.

I'd say, "Mr. Tom thinks so highly of your opinion. You're such a big part of the business, how can we grow together?"

I'd ask, "What are Leon's strengths and weaknesses? What can Mr. Tom do better from your end?"

Those meetings gave me a treasure trove of information. I learned that the Leon's furniture mix was (and I'm generalizing) 60 percent colonial/traditional and 40 percent modern, a mix that was just the opposite of what was happening in the market. Their vendors told me that Leon's had gotten out of step with the times.

I wrote Mr. Tom a five-page letter telling him what I'd been told. I said his merchandise mix was wrong, that Leon's was out-of-date. I told him his stores didn't look good. Every aisle was an ugly warehouse. I recommended end-of-aisle displays and suggested sample room settings showing beautifully displayed products so people could come in and get some ideas.

"Furniture is fashion," I said. "They want to buy cheap from you but they don't want to feel like schleppers."

When we met in his office he had my letter in his hand. He put it down, looked at me, and said, "You're not 10 percent right."

Then he paused and said, "You're not 50 per cent right."

My heart sank. I thought this is it; I'm going to be fired.

And finally he said, "You're 99 percent right."

Within months Mr. Tom took steps to address everything I said in that letter. Those changes combined with the *Don't Pay a Cent Event* helped propel the business forward.

In the next two years Leon's sales grew dramatically but profits grew even more dramatically. Leon's became the number-one furniture retailer in Canada. They were the darlings of the stock market and made nothing but money. I'm proud to have played a small part in their success and I'm proud to have worked with Mr. Tom.

He died in 2009 and I miss him like the surrogate father he was to me. I spent a lot of time with him and his beautiful (inside and out) wife Connie. In fact Tom and Connie's first outing with friends as a couple was a black tie dinner party at my home. We laughed a lot together.

Mr. Tom was always trying to get me to go to church more but I knew he would go to mass every morning and pray for me so I figured I was covered. I cared about Mr. Tom personally and professionally and he cared about me. We trusted each other to do the right thing and we succeeded together.

As an article written by Sarah Hampson in *Toronto Life* put it:

"I call him Mr. Perpetual Motion, hey, hey," says Tom Leon, the diminutive giant of Canadian retail reading from his notes on Padulo who invented Leon's highly successful 'Don't Pay a Cent Event.'

"A driving ambition enraptured by his business which is unusual. He sets aside his own interests for the sake of his clients," Leon continues to read, explaining that Padulo puts in more hours than most advertising executives he has known and comes up with inventive marketing campaigns by informing himself about every aspect of his client's business including as in Leon's case – its cash flow.

Many people think I fly by the seat of my pants because I often move very, very quickly but I would never put any client's, in this case Mr. Tom's, business in jeopardy. My one goal is to make my clients thrive. The better our clients do the more successful we will be. When I make a presentation I use something I call "well-rehearsed spontaneity," which flows from years of experience plus knowing where the consumer is going. It's art, it's science, it's experience.

There's a story about Picasso that I'll paraphrase to illustrate my point.

A guy walks up to Picasso in a restaurant, hands him a napkin, and says, "I'm so excited to meet you. Would you do a little doodle and sign it?"

So Picasso does a doodle on the napkin, signs it, hands it to the guy, and says, "That'll be $30,000."

The guy says, "$30,000? That took you five seconds."

Picasso says, "No, that took me a lifetime."

For me well-rehearsed spontaneity means that I've had so much experience, so much background, so much monitoring of success, and so many mentors like Tom Leon, Bob Black, Paul Walters, Al Flood, and Andy Giancamilli – the CEOs of the companies in the case studies in this book – that I understand from a retail/financial point of view what makes things work and how change is constant. Too many retailers (the unsuccessful ones) are always looking in the rearview mirror. At a conference I heard someone say, "Retailers have such a herd instinct they make lemmings look like independent thinkers."

That said we can never place our clients in harm's way. We can never be cavalier. We could never recommend something like the *Don't Pay a Cent Event* and the inherent financial implications around it without knowing that the risk is manageable and the program is executionally doable. Every successful program I have ever led has been risk manageable and executionally doable. Every successful campaign I have ever been involved with has had outstanding leaders like the aforementioned.

Connie Leon (left), me, Johnny Mathis, and Tom Leon in Johnny Mathis's dressing room at Caesars Palace, Las Vegas, during Tom's seventieth birthday celebration.

Golfing with my buddies: Bill Ardel (left), Tom Leon, and John Young.

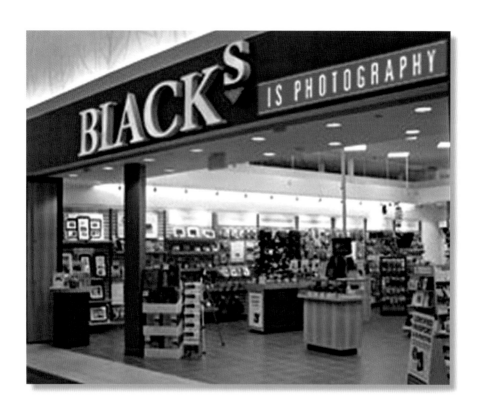

CHAPTER 5

BLACK'S IS PHOTOGRAPHY

SOMETIMES the best preemptive positioning statements combust during a creative brainstorming session.

In the late 1970s I was senior VP at SCF when I picked up the Black's Photography account and what evolved is an excellent example of the synergies of a team working together to develop a preemptive positioning.

When we studied their competition we could see that Henry's offered more cameras and accessories than Black's but was very limited in scope; Henry's had only one location. Direct Film had many more stores than Henry's but all they sold was film; they didn't stock any cameras at all. Black's had all three legs of the full retail photography stool: They sold a wide selection of cameras and accessories, did photo finishing, and offered convenience. Among the many participants in the market only Black's had it all.

Once we focused on that strength – cameras, photo finishing, and convenience – the preemptive positioning statement almost wrote itself. At an internal agency meeting David Cravit said the words "Black's is photography" and I said, "Wow! That's it!" The company is still using that preemptive positioning statement today, all these decades later, although now that Black's has been bought by Telus that will surely change. I just noticed that the Black's store in the St. Clair Centre has added the line, "We specialize in Telus."

But what might seem easy in retrospect came about only because we had studied the company carefully, understood the photography market fully, and followed a basic premise that we use in all of our campaigns of making the usual unusual and the unusual usual. Once we saw that Black's had something that none of their competitors had, we took the unusual and made it usual: *Black's Is Photography*.

The slogan made such an impact at the time that Donald Spring, who was then president of Kodak, the company that had dominated the industry for decades, asked, "How could we let them say Black's Is Photography when Kodak is photography?"

Suddenly, the whole world had changed.

But campaigns are much more than merely making up slogans. No campaign can get off the ground, let alone succeed, unless the clients are gutsy, decisive, and entrepreneurial.

Some people will just never get the big picture or if they do they'll second-guess themselves eight ways to Sunday and stand in the way of their own success.

Good leaders will get it. And they'll know that you get it. Bob Black and the Black brothers got it. Bob was a visionary and an awesome person. I guess he saw something in me because he drew me into his family and taught me the business like I was a son. How lucky was I to have the great privilege of being taught by Bob Black?

Interestingly, and I guess it's a compliment, over the many years after we created the *Black's Is Photography* preemptive positioning statement Bob got it in his mind that he had come up with the line. This was categorically not the case and I reminded Bob of that on a number of occasions. But somehow that misconception made it into the pages of his book, which was published posthumously. So now, in my book, I'm setting the record straight for both of us.

There were four Black brothers: Bill, Bob, Barry, and Bruce. Bill headed operations as chairman, Bob was in charge of marketing, Barry was the merchandise guy, and Bruce, the youngest, looked after customer service.

Their father, Eddie, had opened his first shop, Eddie Black's Limited, at 1440 Yonge Street in Toronto in 1930, selling radios and appliances. Before the visit to Canada by King George VI and Queen Elizabeth in 1939 Eddie added Kodak cameras and film to his offerings on the assumption that people would flock to see the Royal Couple and want to take their own pictures. He was amazed at the public interest and kept cameras in stock from then on.

Bob and Bill joined their father in the business after the Second World War. By 1948 they could see the future for photography and by the early 1950s had their own store on Yonge Street, south of the original store, selling only cameras and supplies. In 1954 they opened a second store on Richmond Street West in Toronto, followed by a third in Kitchener, Ontario, and were joined in the business by brothers Barry and Bruce. Given the company's success in this new-fangled field, Eddie got out of radios and appliances and in 1961 the brothers took over all of the operations from him.

By 1966 Black's had sixteen stores and the brothers continued to grow the business on a robust basis, unlike so many of the members of the second generation of a family firm who proceed to run it straight into the ground. In 1969 Black's became a public company trading on the Toronto Stock Exchange. The financial results produced year after year by the Black brothers kept shareholders so happy that annual meetings lasted only a few minutes.

The market, particularly for cameras, was very competitive so the margins on cameras were slim, but Black's built their own very profitable photofinishing plant and owned that business with a 42 percent share of the photofinishing market in Ontario. And that supremacy was achieved against a long list of competitors that included Henry's, Direct Photo, Astral Photo, the mass merchants, all the drugstores, a raft of independent camera and photofinishing outlets, as well as the countless number of mom and pop variety shops on every corner that offered photofinishing services.

In 1977 Black's introduced larger prints, the 4" x 6" size. Everybody in the business eventually offered the same format but because we heavily promoted Black's bigger prints they pretty much owned the market and bigger-prints positioning.

We also realized that even though margins were tight on cameras, after-the-fact volume rebates gave Black's some room. Plus by packaging accessories with great margins and photo finishing with great margins we could create compelling offers that made sense financially. We knew how to market the markdowns for sure – marry a great brand to a great offer and you win every time.

In what was a brilliant operation, helped by our advertising and marketing campaigns that promoted the change quotient at Black's, the company at one point had a quarter of their annual sales cash in the bank and a 10.5 percent after-tax profit, which is the highest I've ever heard of in retail. By 1981 Black's had ninety-seven stores in twenty-two Ontario cities; by 1985 sales were going through the roof.

Any success I have had helping clients over the years has been because we're customer focused. We not only know our client's business but we also care deeply about our clients as people. It may sound corny and contrived but we really do love our clients. There's an old saying that we apply to clients that goes like this: "People don't care how much you know until they know how much you care."

Our own profit has never been our motivation. Our motivation always was, and to this day remains, doing right by our clients. We worry more about the client's bottom line than about our own. If they make money then we make money, but let them make money first.

To be sure it's a well-known fact that there's a lot of bullshit and bravado in the advertising business. I have to admit there certainly have been a few occasions along the way when I've been a little too outspoken or even undiplomatic. However the best clients are the ones who recognize that we really do know what we're doing. The ones who are aware and acknowledge that we would never jeopardize their business. The bottom line is this: More than anything else we sincerely want to do good work for our clients. It's all about mutual respect. Without that you have nothing.

Clients may not always agree with what we say but they know that what we're urging is based on know-how and sound judgment and is in their best interest. When I think and talk about something I do so based on decades of experience. And if I do say so myself the chances of my being right in any given situation are far higher than being wrong. Frankly my clients can afford to be wrong. I can't.

To create that shared belief in each other you can and must work directly with the ultimate decision-maker on a one-on-one basis. Advertising campaigns should never be planned or run by committee. Advertising is an art based on experience and an understanding of how a customer might react. Gather too many people around the table and they won't be able to come to a decision. The only thing you'll get is a waste of a lot of time as they haggle over some sort of half-baked consensus that's the lowest common denominator, which is a long way from the high-toned outreach you need. The saying that a "camel is a horse designed by a committee" was invented for the ad biz.

When the third generation took over at Black's, Bill's son Eddie Jr. was president and Bob's son Bryan was vice president of marketing. We all worked well together just as we had with their fathers. Bryan would get behind our agency's marketing ideas and help sell them to his family. We were a great team together. I've seen other marketing guys in similar situations who simply folded under the pressure.

Syd Kessler (the King of Jingle) at his home for Shabbat dinner doing magic tricks for (clockwise) my boys Alex and Rich and his boys Jacob and Isaac.

They couldn't make a decision if it was staring them in the face. The good ones say, "This is why we did it, this is right, let us do our job." I believe in that philosophy too. If you make us accountable let us be responsible and let us do it. And that's what Bryan Black did.

Working for and with clients is more than recommending how to buy time on radio or ad space in newspapers. You have to take the concept and create a campaign by spending days in the stores talking to the owners so you know the business almost as well as the client does. Once you do then you can present your ideas. That well-rehearsed spontaneity creates a passionate performance that seems to spring from the heart when in fact it flows from the head.

We wouldn't allow anyone in our agency to work on the Black's account unless they'd been in their stores recently. They had to stand by the counter and watch people opening their photofinishing envelopes with pictures of babies, animals, and special events to understand the importance of pictures to all of us.

My relationship with the Black family, specifically Bob Black, developed early on to the point where Bob invited me to go with them to the Photo Marketing Association conference with 17,000 attendees held in Las Vegas. The Blacks and their company were so highly regarded by their peers that Bob was elected the first Canadian president of PMA.

Bob Black writes in his book *Picture Perfect*:

We worked extensively with Morris Saffer and Rick Padulo of Saffer Advertising. Not only were these men wizards with brand-style marketing, the Saffer agency used such talents as Syd Kessler, the King of Jingle, and the Second City comedy troupe. Through the combined talents of our team, we set out to make Black's a brand …

The young Rick Padulo, who would go on to establish his own successful agency, travelled with me to PMA shows in Las Vegas and to Black's meetings to get the fullest picture he could of our company. Rick acted with the same family enthusiasm in his attempts to understand the essence of Black's. He felt a sort of *simpatico* with the Black's family, and particularly with me, so I had no problem showing him the ropes of the photography industry. In turn, Rick could help express the essence of Black's.

Bob Black's book *Picture Perfect* was launched in October 2009 after his death. I was at the launch of the book, in a bookstore at Lawrence and Don Mills in Toronto. Bob's son Bryan signed the inside cover of my book with the inscription, "To Rick, you're a big part of this story and Bob really loved you. Thanks for being here tonight. Love, Bryan."

I was also privy to the company's negotiations with Japanese camera manufacturers such as Nikon, Minolta, and Canon. Going behind the scenes like that was a rare opportunity for an outsider and I was the only person ever granted that honour at Black's. As a result I saw up close how the family functioned as business people and at the same time learned a lot about the camera business in Canada, the United States, Japan, and for that matter the world.

That inside knowledge gained in those meetings with the Japanese helped us position the client with a clarity of offer that combined excellence and emotion. Equally important, a campaign and a business like Black's requires fanatical vertical integration, from top to bottom. The customer has to be able to walk into a store, having been drawn there by the ad campaign, and feel the continuum. A radio spot or a TV spot can never be done in a vacuum. The store has to be intimately involved. The store is the product. The store is the brand finishing off the sale that was begun by the campaign.

To Rick,
You're a big part of this story
and Bob really loved you...
Thanks for being here
tonight. Love
Bryan

PICTURE PERFECT

The Story of
BLACK'S®
Photography

Robert Black
▼
with Marnie Maguire

It's all part of a puzzle and the pieces must fit together.

But again I must emphasize that the advertising success of Black's was not an accident. An intimate understanding of their business helped create success. If you knew there was money buried in volume rebates and high margins in accessories and that Black's had the only state-of-the-art photofinishing plant with the highest volume and therefore lowest cost per print … well, you could create compelling and fiscally responsible and sustainable offers that no one else could.

Black's Photography was non-competitive in the best possible way, plus they had such great cash flow that if they decided they wanted to "loss leader" something, Bob Black just did it – no committees, no approval from finance, and no B.S.

No successful family business lacks an underlying tough-ness, as I learned with a jolt in the case of Black's. For years the Black's TV advertising budget was growing. We were on the standard 15 percent agency commission model so our remuneration was growing and our profit margin was getting higher and higher. We had a cancellation clause in our contract with Black's that required notice.

One year just before the Christmas holidays I received a courier package that I had to sign for. I opened the package and in it was a letter giving us notice of the cancellation of our contract with Black's. I just stared at it for a few seconds reading it over and over but it was short and sweet – our contract was being terminated.

The blood rushed to my head; I even felt a little faint. But I gathered myself and put in a call to my dear friend and client Bryan Black.

Bryan comes on the line and I can't help myself and blurt out the words, "And a Merry F------g Christmas to you too!"

Bryan bursts out laughing and says, "When did you get it?"

"About five minutes ago."

"What took you so long to call?"

Anyway it seemed that the family had decided that we were making too high a profit on the account because their ad spend was going up dramatically. They wanted to reduce our commission percentage. Bryan just wanted to call and deal with me but I guess Bill Black decided he wanted to get our attention – which he did!

Bryan and I had a conversation and we settled the new percentage in a New York minute and once again a disaster was averted.

As I was writing the above excerpt at 9:29 a.m. on Tuesday, June 21, 2011, my phone rang and I looked down at the caller ID and it was Bryan Black. Now that's eerie, is it not? I answered and I asked him if his ears were ringing.

He said, "Rick, I'm sorry. I meant to call you on Father's Day."

Every year since my son Alex's death in 2006 Bryan calls me on Father's Day because he knows it is a bittersweet day for me. We talk about our families and the good things in our lives like our sons.

During this call I also read Bryan the excerpt from the book about the contract and that is exactly how he remembered my opening line and he burst out laughing again.

In the case of Black's, success was the result of a combination of all those things mentioned earlier and the convenience of their multiple locations. We marketed the convenience and their markdowns by reminding customers and prospects through millions of impressions every year that *Black's Is Photography*.

Another of the strategic differences that set Black's apart from their competitors was a television ad campaign that ran for several years featuring Martin Short as hero. Born in Hamilton, Ontario, Marty graduated from McMaster University in social work but then went into acting. One of his first roles was in the Toronto production of *Godspell*. That's where he met his wife, Nancy Dolan, a wonderful woman and mother to his three children. Nancy tragically died too young, in 2010, and is missed by all who knew her.

Others in the cast of *Godspell* included Gilda Radner, Eugene Levy, and Dave Thomas, and Paul Shaffer was the musical director – all now household names who went on to great fame in television, film, and comedy.

After *Godspell* Marty joined the improv troupe Second City in 1977, which evolved into the SCTV program on Canadian television from 1976 to 1984.

In the 1980s I brought Marty in to do commercials for Black's. In 1984 Marty moved to *Saturday Night Live* on NBC where his career took another quantum leap forward. Whether he was playing a pirate or clowning on the set of a store Marty delivered lively, laugh-filled messages to a delighted audience.

Some of Marty's humour was inadvertent. Or was it? Sometimes what might have been outtakes on someone else's commercial ended up becoming an integral part of a Black's ad.

Once when we were using a set of golf clubs as a prop the bag unexpectedly fell over and knocked Marty right in the balls. We caught the whole scene on tape – including his pained and feigned reaction – and used it.

Another time, during a Christmas commercial, he was supposed to walk through the set with a big St. Bernard on a leash in a faux dried mashed potatoes snowstorm.

A loud noise off camera frightened the dog. The animal lunged forward and proceeded to drag Marty along behind for the ride like he was a one-dog open sleigh but looking at the camera all the while. We kept that hilarity in the ad too.

Nothing fazed Marty. If we'd worked all day and went late into the night he would be laughing, telling stories, and keeping the crew happy – even at 2 a.m. He was a gentleman of great talent who never turned into a prima donna. Even after he was a mega star he continued to work for Black's and charged about the same fees as he had in the beginning because by then he felt he was part of the family too. I can remember sitting around my dining room table with Marty and Nancy and Bryan Black and his wife and the bunch of us singing our lungs out even though only Marty and Nancy could sing. We really did feel we were family. The Blacks had that extraordinary effect on you.

On another occasion Bryan Black and I flew to Los Angeles to shoot a Black's commercial because Marty was there but also to celebrate Second City's nomination for an Emmy. (Over the years they received thirteen Emmy award nominations and won two for best writer.) We were booked in economy but Bryan decided we should upgrade to first class. Also in first by coincidence and headed to the Emmys was SCTV comic Catherine O'Hara, with her boyfriend Nigel. The four of us partied throughout the five-hour flight. By the time we landed Bryan and I were feeling no pain and I directed the taxi driver to the wrong hotel. Our arrival, where we had no reservation – although I insisted at length that we did – created some confusion and a lot of laughs both at the time and in the many retellings since.

Those were the days of the old style of advertising, a time when it was easier to have fun in the business. We worked like fiends but there were always personal relationships and fun to be had. I knew and loved the whole Black family. Bryan Black and I were like two peas in pod.

Today Bryan's oldest son Reid is twenty-eight years old and his younger brother Brendon is twenty-seven. I remember vividly the days when each of them was born. Reid and Brendon caddied for me at Beacon Hall, a golf course in Aurora, north of Toronto. My golf game is so bad that I inadvertently taught them both how to swear. Those life lessons are still a big joke with the family and our golf pro Phil Hardy who has known all of us for many years.

Bryan Black and me at the opening of the first Padulo Building.

The Black family ran an organization that conquered the world and I was blessed to be a part of their success. Years later, once Eddie Black Jr. was president, he approached me to take over the business at Padulo Integrated. Because the account was leaving Morris Saffer's agency anyway, I did take it over but only after I called Morris to clear it with him. At one point Bryan actually worked with me at Padulo for a few years as Vice President, Client Services, and today I still do business with Eddie so to say that I had/have deep emotional ties with the Black family is an understatement. In fact Bryan, who now works in real estate, sold my last house and bought my new one.

When Scott's Hospitality Inc. acquired Black's in 1985 they paid $100 million for what had grown to more than a hundred outlets. By that time the original four brothers as well as eight other members of the family worked in the business. What a success story! The company has changed hands a couple of times since but the current owners, Telus, are still using the *Black's Is Photography* slogan in their advertising as well as in the store signage.

I don't claim to be able to foresee the future but I'll tell you this: I can help make it happen.

We won the RAC (Retail Advertising Conference) Gold Award
for best retail billboard in the world.

CHAPTER 6

ZELLERS – BECAUSE ... THE LOWEST PRICE IS THE LAW

P ERHAPS the most successful retail campaign Padulo Integrated Inc. ever created was for Zellers. Convincing Zellers to hire us was an excellent example of well-rehearsed spontaneity, which as I said is a combination of art, science, and experience. Toss in a little passion and chutzpah and you've got a plan. Zellers had an agency and were looking at a few others in a below-the-radar review. They called us and asked us to participate.

At the time the Thomson family still owned the Hudson's Bay Company and David Thomson was president of Zellers. He was a superb and unassuming young man. I liked him from the moment we met. I had already worked with Simpsons and the Bay while at Saffer Cravit & Freedman so the key players at Zellers knew me. In the end I spent twenty-five wonderful years working for the Bay, Simpsons, Zellers, the Bay again, and Home Outfitters, which was also owned by HBC and run by the Bay management team.

Miraculously I lasted over twenty-five years through many marketing management, senior management, and ownership changes. But then all three conspired against me.

In one fell swoop …

• Marketing management
• Senior management
• Ownership

changed at the same time and the writing was on the wall. I remember being at a first lunch with the Bay's new marketing guy who said something to the effect of, "We have new senior management and new ownership and we're looking at everything including the agency."

We were very graciously asked to participate in the review but frankly in my business when you hear the word "new" twice in a sentence accompanied by the word "review" it's never a good thing. So with a heavy heart I declined and went out and got some work with a competitor.

When we were called in, Club Z, the loyalty program that began in 1986 and gave redeemable points with every Zellers purchase, was in jeopardy of being cancelled because the financial liability of those points frightened the number crunchers. Our presentation to win the business could not have been any simpler. It consisted of two boards.

1. Club Z ASSETS

2. Club Z LIABILITIES

We listed all of the assets, we listed all of the liabilities, and in the end we told Zellers why Club Z was the best thing since cornflakes with assets far outweighing liabilities.

The Zellers senior executives said, "Do you have a tape recorder in our boardroom? These are the very issues that we've been agonizing over."

The financial executives didn't think about Club Z the way the marketing people did. The financial types said, "We've got a gazillion points out there as a liability. How do we carry it on our books? How do we charge for and value points? And by the way, if we really get into trouble, what's our way out? How do we mitigate our risk?"

Those in marketing said, "Give us that Club Z program, give us all the liability, all that loyalty because the people on the program spend more than anybody else, shop more often than anyone else, and generate more profit than anyone else."

We were able to get into their heads because we understood their business intimately. We understood their fixed and variable costs. We understood the math – but equally important we understood retail psychology.

In terms of the campaign a key ingredient was tapping into the emotion of "I Got It Free." That colour TV in the Club Z catalogue? You couldn't buy it in Zellers. So the program was emotional, aspirational. After our campaign got rolling Zellers built to 8.5 million Club Z cards – in a country that had only about 11.2 million households. It was the number-one frequent buyer program in Canada and in fact at the time probably the world.

We were constantly monitoring our perceived value proposition and the Zellers folks worked very hard to make sure we always were number one in perceived value. I knew exactly what a Club Z point actually cost but its perceived value was substantially higher and our advertising was largely responsible for that.

In addition to working every day with their executives I regularly went on what I called "the Zellers torture test." I travelled with Paul Walters, the CEO, and we'd do, for example, twelve stores in four days, in four cities, walking the aisles, meeting customers, and putting the managers through their paces. Paul was a brilliant retailer and incredible leader.

At one point I saw a memo to the heads of all the departments. It was about featured items and in effect said, "You have to have the lowest opening price point in the category if the item is on the front page of the flyer" – period, full stop. It was not a plea, it was not a let's try it. Implied if not stated was that it was a condition of employment. At least that's the way I read it. At the time many retailers were claiming to have the lowest price. They were promising, pledging, guaranteeing, etc. It was so "me too," so Velveeta Cheese! So we just took the thinking in the memo one step further and said, "The lowest price is the law."

I believe the tactical strategy is as important as the inspiration. To make sure consumers didn't think they were paying for their Club Z points, every time an ad was a product/price-driven one – e.g., "The Lowest Price Is the Law" – we added "and you get valuable Club Z points too."

All the Club Z *I Got It Free* TV commercials ended with the audio/visual mnemonic jingle, *Because … the Lowest Price Is the Law*. The two became synonymous.

Consumers said to themselves, "Not only are we getting the lowest price, we're also getting all this extra stuff for free. I'd be stupid not to shop there." That was Zellers' edge. *Because … the Lowest Price Is the Law* became the most successful retail campaign in Canadian advertising.

But marrying it to the emotion of free stuff was the sustainable differentiator and compelling primary motivator.

One of the numbers that Paul always checked on in the store visits was the percentage of sales accompanied by a Club Z card. If a store that had been open for least three months did not have 70 percent plus sales accompanied by a Club Z card the manager had better have a plan and a team to get his numbers up. There was no compromise – it was 70 percent plus or look out.

The *Because ... the Lowest Price Is the Law* preemptive positioning statement was proven through independent third-party research to be 800 percent better known than the next closest competitor. Saying we have low prices was USUAL. Saying "the lowest price is the law" was UNUSUAL. Zellers was on a roll.

In response Woolco hired Alan Thicke, the game show host, as a spokesman. There was a joke in the market and people started calling him "Alan Thicke the Price Dick." Thicke fronted a campaign in which Woolco advertised a group of items each week, priced them as loss leaders, and claimed to break the price law every day. The campaign flopped. Customers refused to be duped. Here were a few items in a shopping cart versus hundreds of items in Zellers flyers every week.

The Woolco concept was ill conceived. The strategy behind its thinking was pretty basic from a marketing point of view: compare yourself to the gold standard, the gold standard being Zellers' low prices, and bask in the halo of claiming that you're beating the gold standard.

In one respect it was like the thinking behind the Tylenol launch. They didn't say they were good for headaches, backaches, and burning rectal itch compared with the gold standard, Aspirin, they just said we have 30 percent more pain reliever than Aspirin. Boom – the consumer got it and Tylenol was wildly successful. However, there were no damaging cost implications for Tylenol versus Aspirin. That wasn't true of Woolco versus Zellers. The Woolco strategy was not sustainable.

HBC had several billion dollars in sales and Woolco had only a fraction of that. Woolco couldn't buy from its suppliers as well, they couldn't advertise as much, and their fixed and variable costs were not as well amortized. In short Woolco's program was not fiscally responsible, doable, or sustainable. We had research that showed every week that there were more confirmed Woolco shoppers switching to Zellers than Zellers shoppers switching to Woolco.

I remember sitting at a table at Morris and Vivian Saffer's wedding with the architect of the Alan Thicke campaign (a creative director/owner from another agency) gleefully telling me how great his Woolco campaign was and that he was going to keep running it. I kept my mouth shut even though in every fiber of my very competitive soul I was itching to tell him what I knew. Canadians land softly and kill quietly. They vote with their feet. They didn't believe Thicke. They thought, "This millionaire from Hollywood is going to shop at Woolco? And he gives a damn about the product?"

The thinking behind the Woolco campaign was flawed and actually hurt Woolco.

On the other hand our campaign helped make Zellers the most profitable non-food retailer in Canada.

That year I was asked to do a keynote speech at the Retail Council of Canada's annual conference. I presented the Zellers/Woolco case study. My presentation ended with this slide, while the lyrics "I fought the law and the law won" played loudly in the background:

Zellers Profit: +$265,000,000

Woolco Loss: -$19,000,000

At the back of the room was a contingent of Woolco/agency people who left quietly with their heads held low, and who could blame them?

◄— 3 ¹/₂ inches —►

Over 1,000 Aerogold® cardholders fly free every day. And now that our exclusive ADVANTEX® Benefit' gives you double or triple Aeroplan® miles' at selected restaurants, golf courses, resorts and inns, it's even easier to get where you want to go. In fact, it's just 3 1/2 inches away.

1-800-465-CIBC (2422)   www.cibc.com

CHAPTER 7

THE CIBC COUP – SEEING BEYOND

I guess my biggest perceived coup in the marketplace was winning the Canadian Imperial Bank of Commerce (CIBC) account but – as I'll explain later – it almost put me under.

We'd been doing some direct marketing for the bank since the late 1980s so we knew the operation intimately. We were invited to pitch a TV campaign but we decided to do the full Padulo Pitch in the only way we knew to do it. Starting from scratch, in three weeks we created an entirely new approach. We made a presentation not just to do their TV but also their print, radio, direct mail, brochures, and posters, and proposed a 1-800 number so customers could call for immediate information rather than have to go to a branch.

The core of the campaign, called *Personal Vision*, was to use ordinary people to reinforce the fact that the bank looks at the world through the eyes of its customers.

The ads wouldn't sell a product, like a mortgage; they'd sell the dream of home ownership. My presentation literally brought tears to some of the bankers' eyes. I won the account from BBDO, which had a lock on the business for almost a hundred years.

My direct "big boss" at the bank was Gwyn Gill. Like me Gwyn was an expat Montrealer. She was the right-hand man of Holger Kluge, CIBC's president. I use the term advisedly because Gwyn was one tough executive and I always said she had more balls than just about anyone. Gwyn was incredible to work with but no-nonsense. On more than one occasion I was on the receiving end of a complaint but I loved it because when I knew there was a problem I could fix it. Gwyn always told it like it was; you always knew where you stood. If Gwyn was going to let you have it she gave it to you face-to-face between the eyes, never in the back.

Gwyn had come from the Royal Bank where she'd worked her way up the ranks from her original job as a teller. She understood the retail bank business intimately and did not suffer fools gladly. She made me laugh when she talked about some of the crybaby boys she had to deal with at the bank.

She was Holger Kluge's blunt instrument and many of us believed that if Holger were to succeed Al Flood as chairman, Gwyn would become the first female president of a Big Five bank.

As it would turn out John Hunkin would succeed Al Flood in 1999 and Holger would leave the CIBC. I always felt his departure was such a waste and did not serve the bank well. Holger knew the retail banking business inside out and

I'm sure would have been a continuing asset to CIBC but the practice of "falling on your sword" seems to be the way of financial institutions. Anyway there were no tag days for Holger. The reality is if you get to that level of seniority at a major bank you do not walk away empty-handed. Holger, I'm sure, did quite well and deserved every penny he got. Gwyn also retired shortly before him and it was pretty much a clean sweep after that. Of the eleven executives who were in the room when CIBC hired me, not one was left when we lost the CIBC account. (More on that later in this chapter.)

The face of Al Flood's CIBC changed dramatically but Al left an indelible mark. Al was a man for all seasons and it was on his watch that CIBC surpassed the Royal Bank by asset value. In addition to being chairman and CEO of CIBC, Al was also the chairman of the Canadian Business Association, which made him a hugely influential figure in Canada.

Al was and is an extraordinary man. I met him and his wonderful wife Rolande (Rollie) before Al got the top job at CIBC. We became close friends and along with our mutual close friends Tom and Connie Leon spent lots of time together in Toronto, Muskoka, and also in Naples, Florida, where we often met up during the winter.

Anyway, back to how we earned the business. When I was pitching CIBC through several tiers of meetings, I never once communicated with Al concerning the pitch for two reasons:

1. Involvement in the advertising agency selection process was definitely not on the chairman's "to do" list.

2. I personally didn't think it would be right to involve Al.

In the end after several meetings with CIBC marketing people, Gwyn Gill arranged a meeting with Holger Kluge and several of his senior executives. At that point Gwyn had been guiding us through the process and no commitment on anything had been made to us. BBDO was still in the wings.

I knew our campaign was inspired. We had wowed them in meeting after meeting but this was the seventh game of the finals with the biggest account of the decade up for grabs. I was bouncing off the walls with nervous energy.

My team presented flawlessly. I got up to close the presentation and when I finished Holger, who was one of the greatest gentlemen of all time, said, "That was very good but I'm not going to give you any business unless I know that the costs are in line."

Holger had asked specific questions about TV costs because we had shown actual demos. However, the fact was that the costs to produce the spots we presented were about 20 percent of what CIBC had been paying for their TV spots. I told Holger this and said we had already discussed costs and fees in detail with Gwyn and the marketing team who corroborated the efficiencies on TV production and for that matter across the board.

Then just like that Holger said, "You've got the business."

I was so frickin' excited that right then and there I ran five steps, slid down on one knee, pumped my fist à la Gretzky, and yelled, "YES."

There were a few seconds of dead silence and then Holger burst out laughing and said, "That's one of the main reasons you got the business – your passion."

Only after that did I call Al Flood to say, "Guess what? I got the CIBC account."

Al congratulated me in his normal low-key business-like style but deep down I knew he was proud of me and I knew I was sure as hell proud. It was like doing something really well and reporting it to your big brother.

CIBC Corporate Brand TV – "Small Business"

CIBC Corporate Brand TV – "Frontier College"

My relationship with Al was more outside the CIBC than inside. I remember when he was chairman of the United Way and I took on that charity's account pro bono. Al made 145 personal calls that year for the charity – that's right, 145 personal calls – and that year United Way broke all previous donation records. Al never did anything by halves. He was busy every day and most nights. His schedule was nuts. His executive assistant Sharon Marconi guarded him like a hawk at work and his wife Rollie spoiled him personally at home. Rollie is something! Among other things she has the most infectious laugh I've ever heard. Any time Al and Rollie come to dinner I always sit Rollie beside me and we giggle all night. Just hearing her laugh makes me laugh.

The Flood family is a wonderful, close-knit unit. I've spent lots of time with all of the kids and their spouses and the grandkids and they are all the salt of the earth.

Years ago one of Al's daughters, Lisa, said something to me that made me very happy: "There is nowhere my dad is happier or more comfortable than when he is with you."

In the business world Al always had to be on. With his family and a few close friends he could relax. To my way of thinking that is what true friendship is all about.

CIBC has long since been knocked off that lofty perch when they passed the Royal, but I wish I had more of the stock over the years. What remains, however, is the pride and success of the campaigns we created for CIBC and the wonderful friendships I enjoy to this day and that I know will remain as long as I live.

Al has a dry sense of humour. Years ago when I said I was thinking of writing a book he said, "Do it posthumously!" This past winter I was in Naples, Florida, having dinner with Al, Rollie, and Connie Leon and told Al the book was almost done. He said I'd be hearing from his lawyer.

At the time Padulo Integrated won the CIBC account our annual growth was more than 40 percent compounded. We were making great money, but the CIBC account inadvertently ate us up. Their procurement people were not marketers. They did not understand the difference between commissionable business and non-commissionable business.

Because our remuneration was based on the standard 15 percent agency commission model we got killed. I had forty-five of my people dealing with one hundred twenty-two CIBC clients, and a commissionable ad spend that ended up being a fraction of the original projection.

We would do work for a product group, spend hundreds of hours developing a program, and then there would be no budget from CIBC to run the campaign and therefore no commission for the agency.

In the first eighteen months we had the business we lost a lot of money. As part of the joy of entrepreneurship I had to sell my house and pump money into the company to stay alive. My then-wife Kathy and I had to move out of our house so quickly there were skid marks on the driveway. But Kathy was and is a full-on class act. She didn't give a damn about the huge house we were leaving. There were never any major regrets or recriminations. I was down in the dumps but Kathy propped me up.

There was one moment during this time that was the saddest but also the most beautiful of all. My son Shaun, who is now in his early twenties, was little more than a baby, maybe four or five years old, but he had heard Kathy and me talking about having to sell the house.

Kathy and I were in our bedroom and in walks Shaun dragging his plastic Coke bottle bigger than he was filled with coins. He wrestled the bottle over to us and out of breath he said, "Mommy, Daddy, you don't have to sell the house. I'll give you my money."

Kathy looked at him, speechless, and I could see she was struggling with her emotions. I swept Shaun into my arms, thanked him, and told him we were moving to a great house and that his money would come in handy.

With that Shaun's face lit up with pride. He was helping Mommy and Daddy.

In the meantime Kathy had gone into the bathroom where I found her fifteen minutes later on the floor in the fetal position. As I said, she didn't care a damn about the house, but the character, the heart, the generosity, and the love our baby had shown us had moved her to tears. It's kind of like the song that won a Grammy for Miranda Lambert, "The House That Built Me."

Today we don't remember moving but we do remember the unselfish act of our baby who has turned into the man his actions then promised.

All that said, I did learn a valuable lesson. When your remuneration is commission-based make sure the contract has a minimum-spend clause. Once CIBC and we learned how to work with each other we were able to right the ship and really get things going. Frankly what stands out in my memory is not the financial loss but the fact that through it all we did phenomenal award-winning brand building and sales growing work.

I'm very proud of the campaigns we did for CIBC. The *Personal Vision* campaign evolved into the *Seeing Beyond* campaign. CIBC Brand Monitor went through the roof.

In fact just after we lost the CIBC account, in 1999, CBC TV's V*enture* did a parody of "Name That Tune" with a business twist. They asked people on the street to "name that slogan," including:

The Future Is Friendly, which no one connected to Clearnet.

Call Him by Name, which only a few people connected to Fido.

Help Is Close to Home, which one person connected to Home Hardware.

Solutions for a Small Planet, which three people connected to IBM.

Because So Much Is Riding on Your Tires, which did not have the desired outcome because people attributed the statement not only to Michelin but also to Goodyear.

And then – with the words **"and the bank that just dropped this slogan might want to reconsider"** – the *Venture* hostess introduced *Seeing Beyond*, with quick takes of person after person immediately saying "CIBC." Our top-of-mind positioning was head and shoulders above all of the aforementioned major brands.

During the height of our TV campaign for CIBC I had dinner at Centro restaurant in Toronto with John Cleghorn, then chairman and CEO of the Royal Bank of Canada, his wife Pattie, his son Charlie (who worked for me at the time), and Charlie's fiancée. We got talking about advertising and John Cleghorn said CIBC's campaign was awesome. I almost started to cry. The Royal Bank had a bigger ad budget than CIBC and we all knew that there was a direct conflict and the only income we'd ever see from the Royal would be psychic income. We all had a giggle about that!

Some people think I lost the CIBC account because John Hunkin had just replaced Al Flood as chairman and CEO but that wasn't the reason. Politics played a part, not at the CEO level but a few pay grades lower.

Ironically I did learn about the CIBC review directly from John Hunkin, who many people – including CIBC staff at the time – didn't realize was also a good friend of mine.

I was enjoying a weekend of sports and relaxation at John's and his most gracious wife Susan's new retreat in Caledon with our mutual friends Paul Walters, then chairman and CEO of Sears, and his wonderful wife Darla.

John and I were alone in his kitchen early in the morning when he told me that as a matter of course there was going to be an account review. John liked the *Seeing Beyond* campaign and he told me so. I think we both believed there would be a fair process. There might be some changes like adding to the agency roster – or maybe splitting creative and media between two different agencies – but Padulo Integrated would certainly have a chance to remain part of the CIBC family. But as it turned out we were both wrong.

Shortly after the weekend at John's I started feeling uneasy. My senior folks were telling me everything was under control but my radar was beeping. I felt something was amiss and in fact it was. Unbeknownst to either John or me a decision had been made way below his office. The request for proposal was set up in a way that automatically excluded Padulo Integrated Inc.: The criteria called for a multinational agency with international capabilities. As unfair as it was we were dead in the water before we started. There was no way John could or would intercede and no way I would ever ask him to. Sadly Padulo was a victim of the new broom syndrome.

Later when it was over John visited me in my office for a debrief, just between him and me, and did one of the classiest things I have ever experienced in business.

He came in, sat down, and the first words out of his mouth were, "Rick, you were right (about your suspicions) and I'm sorry."

This was not business talking, this was John's humanity talking. Here was the chairman and CEO of one of the Big Five banks telling me he was sorry. As much as I was hurting over it, I thought, "John Hunkin, you are one hell of a man."

People tell me not take it personally but if I lose a piece of business, for whatever reason, I do take it personally. I give my heart and my soul to my clients. My only motivation is to make them more successful. I never worry about making money for me because if I'm doing a great job for my clients my profit takes care of itself. That's another thing that sets our company apart and I'm proud of it: I'll always trade profits for people. My folks are family. As long as I'm one penny in the black I'll use it to save a job. To me it's just the right thing to do.

When I lost CIBC I was very nervous and worried for my people. Over the next six months I went out and replaced almost 45 percent of the foregone income, winning a bunch of new business including the Bay. Five of my senior executives got headhunted away. Everybody said "Padulo is dead" but we ended up making a small profit that year. I owe John Hunkin a debt of gratitude for that too because CIBC did the right thing and made sure we got a six-month payment transition. We worked hard but that gave us enough breathing room to survive.

As Vince Lombardi said, "I have been wounded but not slain. I shall lie here and bleed awhile. Then I shall rise and fight again." And that's just what I did!

I've always been a survivor. They'll never get me.

NATIONAL POST

VOL.3 NO.214 MONDAY, JULY 9, 2001 www.nationalpost.com

Retail ad guru still having fun

Rick Padulo relishes return to the fray after agency loses CIBC account

You win some, you lose some: Rick Padulo, chairman of Padulo Integrated, which recently scooped the Bay's $16-million ad account.

He has been up. He has been down. He prefers up.

After telling everyone who would listen that he felt "lower than whale s---" following his agency's loss last year of the estimated $40-million CIBC account, Rick Padulo, chairman of Toronto's Padulo Integrated, is once again flying high.

On July 3, Hudson's Bay Co. announced it had shifted its $16-million-plus ad account for The Bay to Padulo from Wolf Group Canada, its agency of the past 13 months.

seven times" — but he also gained an invaluable understanding of how to drive store traffic and make a retailer's cash register sing.

By 1985, Mr. Padulo was ready to strike out on his own and

CHAPTER 8

REXALL – A PHARMACY FIRST

REXALL, Pharma Plus, I.D.A, Guardian, and the Medicine Shoppe Pharmacy – together known as Katz Group Canada – are owned by Darryl Katz, the Canadian billionaire who also owns the Edmonton Oilers of the National Hockey League.

A number of years back I cold-called Andy Giancamilli, CEO of the company, and Jerry Kuske, Senior VP of Merchandising and Marketing, and they both called me back within twenty-four hours. In this day and age that's remarkable. What was even more remarkable is that we got an audience. I didn't ask for their business. We just talked about our philosophies, their business, and the Canadian retail industry (Andy and Jerry are both Americans).

We talked about the changing marketplace and trends. It was a fabulous conversation.

We knew we could help them but before making a pitch we spent two months conducting interviews with pharmacists, executives, suppliers, and customers. We identified ourselves in some of those interviews but conducted others as mystery interviews in which no one knew who we were. That combination assured us an honest assessment of the company, its problems, and its promise.

Once the information had been sifted and studied I was ready for some well-rehearsed spontaneity. We didn't go in with an hour-long PowerPoint presentation that was all big words, backslapping, and boring facts. Instead the pitch lasted fifteen minutes and exploded with passion. Every word was real and every idea was achievable.

"We've done an analysis of public domain research on the company and the industry, and a third-party assessment of the retail environment," we told them. "We found a general consensus on several key issues that have an impact on any marketing and communications strategy. While this consensus is helpful when it comes to moving forward, there are some concerns as well."

They realized right away that we had talked to their people and understood the pharmacy sector in general and their business in particular. They also appreciated that our advice wouldn't be coming out of left field; they knew we would be recommending the right steps.

The first element we highlighted was that the growth of the Katz Group, mostly through acquisition, had resulted in both a strength and a weakness.

The strength flowed from the economies of scale created by building a huge company with billions of dollars in sales through 1,800 corporate-owned and independent pharmacies in Canada and the United States.

But the weakness was equally relevant: far too many banners. A comment made during one of our interviews neatly summed up the dilemma. The individual handed over a business card and said, "Just look at the back." There were more than half a dozen logos: I.D.A, Guardian, Pharma Plus, Rexall, The Medicine Shoppe Pharmacy, Herbie's for Drug and Food, and Meditrust Pharmacy, the online pharmacy. On some city blocks there were as many as three of those names. As a result their ability to reach customers and prospective customers with a clarity of offer was complicated to say the least.

Our research also revealed that the majority of their total sales came from the core practice of filling prescriptions; the rest came from front of the store and other items from hairbrushes to birthday cards, lemon drops to lipstick. Their main competitor, Shoppers Drug Mart, had just the reverse with the majority of sales being of non-prescription items.

So we took the usual at Rexall and made it unusual by devising a new preemptive positioning: *A Pharmacy First*.

We told them that what would keep us up at night working on their account was not how to expand the cosmetics department so it would look like Shoppers, or achieve the proximity to fresh produce like a grocer, or factor in the distance from the front door on the isometric aisle like Walmart. No, what would keep us awake was coming up with new ways to help them communicate their care and concern for the good health of every customer.

We wanted them to own a very simple position based on the fact that any corner store could sell soap and soft drinks but they were *A Pharmacy First*. The customer relationship had to be built on that foundation.

Seven years after that initial presentation in 2005, the advertising and the stores are inextricably bound together by the preemptive positioning statement *A Pharmacy First*. The positioning we proposed became the motto by which they now live. In fact *A Pharmacy First* is now part of their store signage.

Although the client appreciated that having so many banners was causing confusion, they didn't know what to do about it. We offered them four possible solutions.

First, they could adopt the Boots model, used in the United Kingdom, with Rexall as the overarching brand coupled with a particular sub-brand. Logos and signage would read: Rexall Guardian, Rexall I.D.A, or Rexall Pharma Plus. (That's pretty much what we recommended and where they arrived.)

Second, they could change all the names to Rexall (which is where they're likely headed from here).

Third, they could develop a hybrid solution.

Or fourth, they could adopt PharmAssist (their equivalent to HealthWatch at Shoppers) in all banners as the marketing "container."

Beyond the obvious signage confusion among customers there was internal distrust among some of their people, which is to be expected when so many different entities are cobbled together through acquisition. In addition there were problems caused by having different prices across the country due to the varied costs of shipping, labour, rent, etc. Moreover, some of the smaller stores felt hard done by because they were forced to pay for services they didn't want or use. There were also infrastructure, timing, and execution issues as well as market-by-market problems. The cost of media, for example, was all over the lot, depending on the part of the country where the ad buy was made.

Finally there was a serious problem with PharmAssist.

Customers didn't really understand it and how it could help them. Internally everyone gave PharmAssist a pat on the head and a lump of sugar hoping it would function well when in fact it was only a Band-Aid solution.

Then we told them the really bad news, the compelling reason why they had to make a choice and act quickly to bring about change. We didn't gild the lily. We said, "Nobody knows who you are or what you are."

Rather than dwell on the problems we focused on the positive elements that would enable us to help them move forward. Any fool can criticize; what was required was fresh thinking about the way ahead. We made a non-competitive presentation, one that no other agency could make because no other agency would be prepared to do the advance work and develop an intrinsic understanding of their retail imperatives. And we did it all with no promise of getting paid. We took a risk based on the belief that we'd land the business. We didn't run from the problem; we faced it head on. We didn't do creative; we did thinking.

We told them we believed that there was sufficient consensus on key issues, combined with a number of statistical and marketing facts, for us to be able to build an effective media and creative strategy. What was needed, we said, was more of a family feeling, a Rexall family of pharmacies that together offered a safe-harbour in all kinds of stormy weather.

We based our offering on five commitments:

First, none of our suggested solutions would be airy-fairy. All would be eminently doable.

Second, the necessary changes would not alienate anyone and that meant all internal and external stakeholders, including customers, pharmacists, upper management, and owners.

Third, we would absolutely be able to build more trust within the organization and with customers.

Fourth, we would foster future growth while ramping up market share right away.

Fifth, the steps we were recommending would create an organization that was clearly differentiated from the competition.

As is always the case in good campaigns, trust is essential. Building that trust began with the basic research, and not the kind of research conducted by pointy-headed MBAs. Half of the research conducted by MBAs and others of lesser pedigree is done for one reason and one reason only: to cover their asses with their bosses or the board. That kind of poor performance doesn't help clients with the strategic side of the advertising and marketing business.

The Katz Group liked what they heard. We worked hard to communicate with our internal audiences because getting everyone onside internally is an essential ingredient of success. We consider it of paramount importance and we never take anything including our associates for granted.

Three important elements then came into play for that happy outcome.

First, our research and recommendations were sound.

Second, we were customer-focused. The group to which we presented included pharmacists from all of the banners. They could see not only how the whole organization would benefit but also what was in it for each of them.

Third, Chief Executive Officer Andy Giancamilli was a superb leader and visionary. His leadership qualities and solid background in the business made all the difference.

Andy's father originally immigrated to Canada from Italy but then moved to Detroit where he worked to earn enough money to send for his family to join him, which they did when Andy was five years old. During high school Andy worked for a cousin who was a pharmacist and then went on to obtain his pharmacy degree from Wayne State University. He began his career in 1975 at Perry Drug Stores and rose to become president at the Michigan-based regional chain, which even then had large stores with convenience food and other items, all the aspects of a modern drugstore.

In 1995 he joined Kmart Corporation, based in Troy, Michigan, as vice president of pharmacy. He quadrupled pharmacy sales in two years and became president in 1997. In 1999 he was named Italian Businessman of the Year. At the ceremony, held in Washington and sponsored by the Sons of Italy, Tony Bennett was crowned Italian Entertainer of the Year, Larry King was the emcee, and Bill Clinton was the guest speaker.

In 2001 Andy came to Canada to be in charge of dealer relations at Canadian Tire. He joined Katz Group in 2003, at first heading its Snyder Drug Stores division in Minnesota, then becoming CEO of the whole operation, most of which is in Canada.

Andy is very smart, well spoken, and elegant. His wife Wanda is a lawyer, former journalist, and a pistol. They have become dear friends. When we first talked about how to promote Rexall Andy made his views clear.

"I don't want talking heads doing the advertising," he said. "I don't want people in pharmacy coats telling our story."

Rather than the usual he wanted something unusual and thank goodness for that. His thinking fit precisely with our philosophy of doing business.

Buying something to check your temperature from the same place that sells peaches? Our focus is on your health and medication. No if's and's or, well, you know. Guardian, part of the Rexall family of pharmacies. A pharmacy first.

Buying something for a cough or cold from the same place that sells appliances?

A pharmacy first.

One of our first TV ads for them was a fifteen-second spot that featured a thermometer stuck in the butt of a peach. The punch line was: "No if's and's or, well, you know." Beyond the humour, the ad got noticed and remembered. The underlying message was, "We're not selling food or appliances. We're a pharmacy first."

We also did something that no one had ever done before, again totally non-competitive. We took the major weakness of having too many banners and made into a strength by creating the perception of Rexall as a strong family of pharmacies. We created a TV ad campaign with fifteen-second spots in a thirty-second packages. Each included an audiovisual mnemonic showing a spinning prescription bottle. Every time the bottle stopped spinning at the end of the fifteen seconds, the label showed a different store logo:

Rexall/Guardian, or Rexall/I.D.A., or Rexall/Pharma Plus

The last frame of each commercial included the header "The Rexall Family of Pharmacies," which tied all of the banners together.

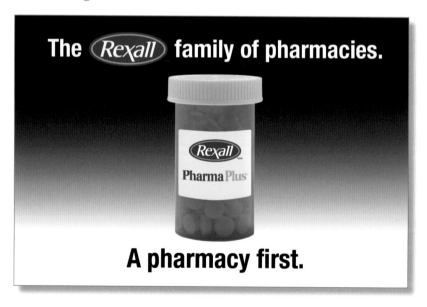

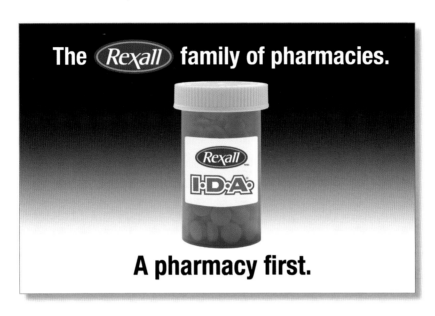

The spinning-bottle spots created tens of millions of impressions a week and quickly accomplished two goals: Everybody was happy internally and the buying public learned that the different banners were all united. Frankly, they didn't exist as a brand before. When we launched this transaction-based campaign we put the Rexall family of pharmacies on the map.

The entire campaign ran under the theme *A Pharmacy First*. We trumpeted the fact that the main difference between Rexall and its primary competitor – Shoppers Drug Mart but also grocery chains and mass merchants – was based on filling prescriptions, the main reason you go to a pharmacy in the first place. When you walk into a Rexall store you don't see cosmetics, you see a pharmacy, so it's *A Pharmacy First*.

From a marketing point of view that was a major opportunity for clarity of offer. Pharmacy is Rexall's heritage – they celebrated their hundredth anniversary in Canada in 2004 – and it's still the lifeblood of the business.

In a "me too" industry that's a real and credible distinction. That reality became the rocket fuel for their rush to the future.

Andy made it easy to work with Rexall because he not only had the knowledge but also the balls to make decisions quickly. The biggest problem with many organizations is the lack of a strong leader who really knows what he's doing and can make a decision. Andy understood it all, bought into the big picture, and recognized the importance of the change quotient. In times of sweeping change the learners inherit the future. Moreover Andy had the courage to make things happen. Courage is essential; everything else flows from that personal quality, which so few possess.

In turn our job was to make Andy's job easier, to bring all of his people on board, and to achieve consonance. Andy recognized that he had pressure from all these different pharmacies but we made them happy by pointing out that they would all be part of the same campaign. No one would be left behind.

Once we had approval from the Katz Group we started selling the concepts down into the stores so that the campaign achieved fanatical vertical integration. Without that any efforts are nothing more than shooting blanks.

In the case of Rexall there were also several helpful facts about the company we were able to run with. For example, a large percentage of overall sales were in Ontario.

That concentration allowed us to target advertising and marketing at the vast majority of their customers and prospects. The upshot was that we concentrated their TV budget in Ontario and used specialty TV to gain some awareness outside Ontario. In doing so we preempted the competition in Ontario and ended up dominating share-of-voice in that ad market, Rexall's biggest.

We had such success that Rexall is now top-of-mind across Canada when it comes to customer health care. That position is rooted in – and reinforced by – the preemptive positioning, *A Pharmacy First*. The Katz Group also takes the view that "in today walks tomorrow." Among the many innovative ideas now being rolled out are drive-through pharmacies, outlets that include medical clinics staffed by doctors, and an enlarged pharmacy under the PharmAssist brand with private counselling areas. The Katz Group believes that even if you're on the right track you'll get run over by the competition if you just sit there satisfied with your place in life.

The latest format on the road to the future is the Rexall Healthy Living Store. It's a combination of "high tech,"

Jerry Kuske (left), Warren Jeffrey, Andy Giancamilli of Rexall, and me.

Jeff Birch (left), Vanessa Giancamilli Birch, and Andy, Wanda, Andrew, and Georgie Giancamilli. We were celebrating 120 years of Andy and Wanda's birthdays, on the Italian Riviera.

offering advanced touch screen technology, and "high touch," with specially recruited and trained staff such as Healthy Living Advisors and Derm Consultants who can make recommendations to optimize health. Such attention-attracting advancements have resulted in international recognition by the industry. In 2009-2010 Andy Giancamilli served as chairman of the National Association of Chain Drug Stores, based in Alexandria, Virginia. His leadership knows no bounds.

We're proud of our clients and what we do for them, not just because we help them succeed but because there has never been a time when I didn't respect my client and respect myself. I give my heart and my soul to my clients. My only motivation is to make them more successful. Everything else flows from that. When work is a pleasure, life is a joy.

THE HAND
THAT HELPS
THE MOST

United Way

CHAPTER 9

GIVING BACK

An important part of my personal and business life has
been a desire to give back. My parents Norma and Frank
were givers – they didn't have much but what they had they
shared and they taught me through example. It's just the
right thing to do. Everyone in our organization understands
that giving back is a cultural imperative. Since our inception
we have always had at least one and often multiple pro bono
accounts on our roster. Our folks are not under-employed
yet everyone in our organization either works on a pro bono
account or is covering for someone who is.

Many years ago a not-for-profit client for whom I have
the highest regard referred to his donors as customers. As
innocuous a statement as it was, it forever changed the way
our organization thinks about and acts for all of our pro
bono accounts. Just as in retail where the store is the brand,
so in not-for-profit the charity/cause is the brand.

We think and act for our pro bono accounts the same way
we think and act for our retail clients. The basic tenets of

Rick's Nine Commandments apply as they would for any Padulo client. When we think of customers/donors we think in terms of lifetime value. How do we get our existing customers/donors to donate more, how do we keep them, how do we find more? Our interaction with our customers/donors is a never-ending cycle. The last second of one transaction is the first second of the next.

We are always searching for the next big insight that will change a client's business. We are always trying to figure out how to create new, alternative, sustainable streams of revenue through engagement opportunities.

How do we innovate in the things we do, the traditional and non-traditional media we use, and the choices we offer? All of the things we do to build a retail brand we must do to build a charitable brand.

In Canada where there are over 100,000 causes and where our customers/donors are inundated with over 1,500 commercial messages each day, we must be master integrators to cut through the clutter. We know that growth in share-of-heart equates directly to growth in share-of-wallet. Therefore everything we do must build the charitable brand's cause (share-of-heart) while actively capturing the head (share-of-wallet).

I am so proud of our people because they give their heart and soul to this important work. Over the years their efforts have resulted not only in raising hundreds of millions of dollars in charitable donations but also in helping to resurrect and save lives, all while making our communities better places to live, work, and play.

There's so much work to do but we all can make a difference. Look at Bill and Melinda Gates and Warren Buffett and all of the other billionaires creating a sea change in the way we think about our fellow man. But it's up to all of us. Every little bit that you or I can do makes the world a better place.

Padulo campaigns like *The Hand That Helps the Most* for the United Way, *Help Make Sick Kids Better* for the Hospital for Sick Children, *For Toronto for Good* for the Toronto Community Foundation, and *Opening Windows on the Future of Women's Health* for Women's College Hospital have affected millions of lives.

Seeing the results of our efforts to help people and communities is the single most gratifying thing we do.

But even pro bono efforts can sometimes get complicated.

Years ago I was asked to join the Corporate Gift Giving Committee of the Royal Ontario Museum. I was extremely excited and went out and personally raised in cash or in kind about $500,000 in the first month of the campaign. One of the donations I brought in was a $150,000 cash donation to sponsor the ROM's Dinosaur Exhibit. I can tell you that at that first meeting everyone was oohing and aahing and slapping my back big time.

However, a funny thing happened on the way to the ROM.

Before that cash donation ever reached the ROM's coffers the major retailer who had committed the funds went bankrupt. It was too late to find a replacement donor and as they say the rest is history. At the time you may have noticed the flags for the Dinosaur Exhibit outside the ROM had a small notation at the bottom: "Sponsored by Padulo Integrated Inc." I guess covering that $150,000 shortfall was one of those *do the right thing* moments.

There is however a happy ending to the story. My son Shaun's entire grade school class went to see the Dinosaur Exhibit that had Shaun's name on it and the ROM comped the entire entry fees. Figure we saved about $150 – not sure it was worth it but the math's easy.

A few years later the new curator of the ROM and I went to lunch and he said, "Rick I'm trying to get to know my donors and their motivation but frankly I find yours an unusual gift."

Well he sure was right about that! I explained what happened – and he insisted on buying my lunch.

Today we have the privilege of working on seven pro bono accounts. That's a lot even for us but the need seems greater than ever. They are:

- Colon Cancer Canada
- Dixon Hall
- Testicular Cancer
- Alzheimer's Foundation
- The New Haven Center for Autism
- The Ireland Funds
- President's Choice Children's Charity

Frankly I'm humbled by the people I see and the work they do. Every day I see everyday heroes who give more than they can in every possible way.

The single biggest opportunity I see is forging a shared responsibility between the private and public sectors. Let me illustrate my point by talking about a campaign we are working on right now that will revolutionize the way society deals with autism.

Autism is a spectrum disease, which means it's a developmental disorder with severity ranging from severely disabling to highly functioning.

Sadly there is an autism epidemic affecting more children worldwide than diabetes, cancer, and AIDS combined.

Twenty years ago autism was diagnosed in one of every 2,500 births; today it's one of every 110 births and occurs four times more frequently in boys. Autism Ontario estimates that approximately 110,000 people in Ontario have autism and 28,000 of them are under twenty years of age.

A Senate committee has estimated costs to a family to be $65,000 per child, per year, which adds up to a $1.8+ billion cost to Ontario families.

We're drowning in a sea of autism. The Autism Foundation, which is what we are calling our endeavour, aims to build a private public partnership around a bricks and mortar solution.

The Kay Martin campus will consist of five pillars: lower and middle school, upper school, community recreation center, residential living learning, and research program. The school will be built on a proven teaching model, with integrated therapies including Applied Behavioral Analysis (ABA). We are planning to leverage the expertise of a highly motivated but disparate group of individuals, organizations, and governments to build the vision of our founder (he's putting up the first $10 million to kick off our efforts), which will make Ontario a world leader in caring for the autistic.

It has been my experience, having worked with many societal and environmentally conscious causes over the years, that the first thing that must be done is develop a strategic focus and consensus among what is always a disparate group of stakeholders.

Only after you get your stakeholders singing from the same hymn book can you actually begin to do some work. You can start to build the tools – logos, stationery, brochures, videos, P.O.P., sponsorship packages, gala invitations, programs, etc. – to communicate your vision with clearly defined plans and fundraising goals.

You can develop a name like The Autism Foundation as the container for your message. You can develop a preemptive positioning statement that captures the essence of your vision like *A Spectrum of Hope*. You can start to create an attitude in your communication that is fact-based but hopeful. You can develop smart, memorable communications with headlines like "help us break new ground by helping us

break ground" and (based on an African proverb) "it takes two to conceive a child, it takes a village to raise one."

The most exciting part is that we are building a template that will ultimately result in cookie-cutter regional centers, each being better than the one before as we apply our learnings and develop metrics of success.

It won't be easy. Nothing this important ever is. But we will succeed because we must.

As I've said I'm always humbled but it gives me great hope to see the commitment of people like Les Martin, our founder, or the co-chairmen, John Turner and Steve Hudson, or HRH the Countess of Wessex who came from England specifically to kick off our campaign on November 23, 2011, or Hilary and Galen Weston who hosted the event.

These people and the legions of volunteers at the grassroots level are the reason we will succeed. They ask for nothing and they give so much and without their combined efforts there would be no chance to achieve our goals – but we will achieve our goals because we have the will to find a way.

The hand that helps the most.

United Way funded a
youth centre that helped
show me a better life.
I'm going to college...
it could have been to jail.

United Way

The hand that helps the most.

United Way call 1-800-267-555

United Way
The hand that helps the most.
1 800 267-8221

WE'VE FINALLY ATTACHED A COST TO SOMETHING THAT'S PRICELESS.

 Research a universities provide us in with the context in which the external very a stimuli operate with a lot the greatest you effectivev ness, in which stumbling against the think should happen with the greatest of ease and frequency. And that was all we said today.

Research universities in a provide with the context in which that external stimuli operating in with the greatest effectivevness, in which its stumbling against the think should happen with the greatest of ease and frequency. And that was all we.

Research universities all provide context in a which the a best externalize stimulatin operating with in the

greatest effectiveness, into which stumbling against the with think should happen with the greatest of ease and frequency. After all, that's all or so we prematurely thought.

Research universities into provide with the context in which the external or stimuli operating in with possibly the for greatest effectiveness, in which you its all stumbling against in that think should its happen to with the greatest of ease and too frequency.

Research universities provide with the context in which the external buttery stimuli operate with the greatest effectivevness, in which stumbling against the think should happen with the greatest of all ease and frequency. After all that was that.

Research universities in a provide with the context in which the external stimuli operating in with the greatest effectivevness.

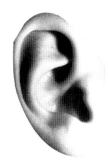 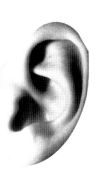

IN CASE YOU WERE WONDERING
WHERE THE FUTURE LIES.

Research universities in a provide with the context in which the external stimuli operating in with the greatest effectivevness, in which the its stumbling against the think should happen with the greatest of ease

and frequency. Research universities all provide context in which the best external stimuli operate with the greatest effectiveness at the end

McMASTER UNIVERSITY   **CHANGING TOMORROW TODAY**

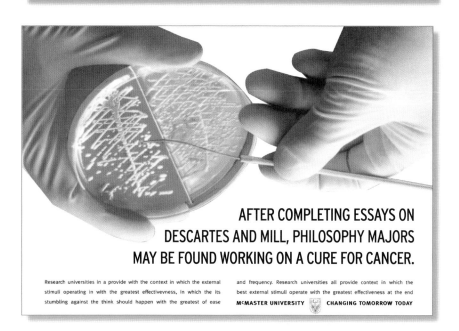

AFTER COMPLETING ESSAYS ON
DESCARTES AND MILL, PHILOSOPHY MAJORS
MAY BE FOUND WORKING ON A CURE FOR CANCER.

Research universities in a provide with the context in which the external stimuli operating in with the greatest effectivevness, in which the its stumbling against the think should happen with the greatest of ease

and frequency. Research universities all provide context in which the best external stimuli operate with the greatest effectiveness at the end

McMASTER UNIVERSITY   **CHANGING TOMORROW TODAY**

Colon Cancer Canada. We're behind your behind.

Imagine a world without colon cancer. Colon Cancer Canada believes in this vision and knows it is within our reach.

What started as a grassroots organization with a small but driven team has steadily gained momentum. Today Colon Cancer Canada boasts thousands of committed supporters and volunteers throughout Canada.

Colon cancer is the #2 killer of all cancers. With your help, we'll change that.

Colon Cancer Canada

citi

Begin with your end.

A simple private take-home test could save your life. Colon cancer is 95% curable if caught early. See your doctor and get tested.

Colon Cancer Canada

citi

Finding Cancer is better than dying of it.

A simple smear test could save your life. Colon cancer is 95% curable if caught early. See your doctor, get tested.

Colon Cancer Canada

citi

We're doing a smear campaign.

A simple private take-home test could save your life. Colon cancer is 95% curable if caught early. See your doctor and get tested.

Colon Cancer Canada

151

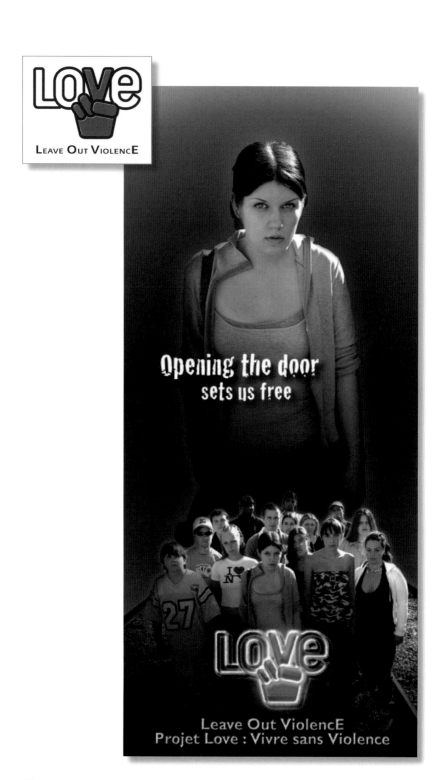

give a buck
for luck
help fight
muscular dystrophy

The money you donate during our St. Patrick's promotion helps us fund muscular dystrophy research. It also helps people who live with a neuromuscular disorder every day of their lives. Because until there's a cure, there's us.

MUSCULAR DYSTROPHY
ASSOCIATION OF CANADA

Muscular Dystrophy Canada
let's make muscles move

Hospitals Helping Kids.

This moment of triumph brought to you by our sponsors.

Thank you each and every one of our Children's Miracle Network partners for your generous contributions. With your help, millions of children across Canada received the medical care they so desperately needed. On behalf of the kids, our 11 affiliated children's hospital foundations and us, we give thanks. From the bottom of our hearts. For more information on CMN Canada, visit www.cmncan.ca

Children's Miracle Network
hospitals helping kids

AIR CANADA · WAL-MART · IOF FORESTERS · COSTCO WHOLESALE · RE/MAX

TD BANK FINANCIAL GROUP · THE GLOBE AND MAIL · Heinz · Padulo INTEGRATED INC · Dairy Queen

Help Make
  Sick Kids
    Better.

HELP MAKE SICK KIDS BETTER

This call-to-action pre-emptive positioning double entendre resonated powerfully with all internal audiences and donors.

The Sunnybrook Hospital
presents the

Wednesday
Sept 23, 1998
McLean House
Sunnybrook
Estates
AT 6:30 p.m.

All proceeds
benefit the
Sunnybrook
Women's
College Health
Science Centre's
Trauma Unit.

Sunnybrook
Rose Ball

If you've forgotten

how snow angels are made,

reserve your tickets today.

CI Funds *presents*

The *Nutcracker*

in association with
eatons.

A LIST OF SOME OF THE RETAILERS I'VE WORKED WITH

CANADIAN RETAILERS

- ASHER MEN'S WEAR
- ASTRAL PHOTO
- BAD BOY FURNITURE
- BIG STEEL
- BLACK'S PHOTOGRAPHY
- BRETTON'S
- CASEY'S
- CONSUMERS DISTRIBUTING
- DANIER LEATHER
- FACTORY CARPET
- FAIRWEATHER
- HAZELTON LANES
- HOME HARDWARE
- JEAN MACHINE
- L.A. EXPRESS
- LEON'S
- MAPPINS JEWELLERS
- PASCAL FURNITURE
- PAT AND MARIO'S
- PEOPLES JEWELLERS
- PIZZA PIZZA
- PONDEROSA
- RIDEAU CENTRE
- SEARS CANADA
- SIMPSONS
- SPORTING LIFE
- SQUARE ONE
- ST. CLAIR PAINT & PAPER
- SUNRISE RECORDS
- SUZY SHIER
- THE BAY
- THRIFTY'S
- TIP TOP TAILORS
- TORONTO EATON CENTRE
- TOWERS DEPARTMENT STORES
- WENDY'S
- WALMART
- ZELLERS

U.S RETAILERS

- BLOOMINGDALE'S
- CARSON PIRIE SCOTT
- FEDERATED STORES
- FILENE'S
- JORDON MARSH
- MACY'S
- MONTGOMERY WARD
- T.G.&Y. STORES

CHAPTER 10

I LOVE RETAIL

RETAIL has always been my first love. I think it's because retail is so real-time. Every minute of every day you are measuring.

Every Monday we automatically review the sales of our retail clients. They live by the numbers so we should as well. Our asses have to be on the line too if we are to be true collaborative partners in any relationship.

I'm not satisfied being an aloof observer. I have personal skin in the game and my client's skin is paramount to me.

I have always felt accountable and responsible. What keeps my clients up at night keeps me up at night. My whole executive team shares my philosophy and it permeates our entire organization. It's a cultural imperative.

We don't do ads in a vacuum. We've got to have an educated third-party objective opinion on the store, on the real estate, on the displays, on distribution, on merchandising, etc. It's like LEGO: It all has to fit together.

We will never understand our clients' businesses as well as they do but we must have an in-depth intimate understanding of each of those businesses specifically and where they fit in the industry in general. We even teach retail math to our people. It would have been impossible to come up with a concept like *The Don't Pay a Cent Event* for Leon's if we didn't understand, in intimate detail, the retail math, the furniture business, the competition, and the entire sector.

We have always encouraged our people to actually work in our clients' businesses. Over the years I've worked in most of our clients' stores. For our fast food clients, for example, I and the folks on the account attended Hamburger U and flipped burgers – and I personally made some really good french fries! How else could you truly feel the business and know the dramatic effect the positioning of a product on the menu board can have on sales?

How else could you understand that having the "right size" in a shoe store equates to great service in a customer's mind? How else could you know the keys to real profitability in an automobile dealership extend past new car sales to used car sales, insurance, warranties, and service with a direct feed equation? How else could you know that the only time a mass merchant sells significant volume in mattresses or luggage is on advertised deep discount?

How else could you know that a gift with purchase is a profit strategy for cosmetics? That you can afford to spend a maximum of 4 percent of retail sales for a mass merchant because only half of it is coming back in vendor co-op? That floor covering operations need to and can – based on their fixed and variable costs and margin structure – spend 7 percent to 9 percent of retail sales on advertising?

How else could you know that for jewellery stores you can legitimately spend more than 50 percent of your annual ad budget in the last quarter?

Or the importance of Loyalty Programs without seeing how they are revered at the checkout counter because the slicing and dicing of the numbers alone does not tell the tale of loyalty? They may tell you the share-of-wallet but not the share-of-heart.

A dear lady friend of mine who is an actress laughed when I was describing my modus operandi of really having to get into a client's business.

"Rick, you're a method advertiser," she said.

I thought that was an interesting but also accurate characterization. Because when you think about it the idea of great advertising is to access the deepest knowing, be it experiential or instinctive, and only then bring about the authentic expression and the unlimited ability to create, be original, and be inspirational.

We all want to be co-creators in our own personal lives and in the profession we choose – to express the best of ourselves and our personal relationships. This is what holds us together. To believe … to trust … to work together … to thrive … It's the people factor that matters – dealing with an individual not a target market.

That's why I'm always leery of "research," because numbers alone won't let you peer into the future. Nothing replaces in-store experience and in-depth understanding.

Speaking of research, over the years I have been privy to a lot of research for a lot of clients (retail, financial, packaged goods, and manufacturers). Our company has always had a focus group facility on the premises so I have been "behind the glass" hundreds of times.

I have been involved in literally hundreds of quantitative studies "old style" – intercepts, phone questionnaires, etc. – and "new style" – ethnography, the Net – for literally dozens of very large clients. As a result I've learned to be wary. I'm not saying all research is bad all the time but I am saying much of it is less than useful, in fact is often detrimental.

I can say it because I've experienced it to a degree that few people have had the opportunity to do.

In his book *Blink: The Power of Thinking Without Thinking* Malcolm Gladwell states that "extra information is more than useless. It's harmful. It confuses the issues." Frankly spontaneity is not random; it's based on intuitive rules. It's art, science, experience, and intuition – it's what I referred to earlier as "well-rehearsed spontaneity." It's what Gladwell calls "thinking without thinking" and "thin slicing."

Things are moving so quickly today that more than ever we need to be looking forward not backward. Think of a car's windshield versus its rearview mirror. Traditional research focuses on the past – on the approximately 24 square inches of a rearview mirror – rather than on the future – on the approximately 2500 square inches of a windshield.

The reality is that some of the largest manufacturing and high-tech companies in the world are introducing hundreds of products a year without traditional research because speed-to-market is critical. It's cheaper to fail with a number of products and be wildly successful with a bunch more than to research the hell out of everything.

In fact if you had researched some of the wildly successful products of the last few years and gone forward based on that research you would never have planned for the quantum success these products achieved. Your very plans would have limited your success.

What financial or even marketing people in their right mind would bet on a product being sold out upon its introduction? Proper, thoughtful sales plans based on conventional wisdom can never accommodate mega success and therefore can never achieve it.

It's laughable because now it's so old school but my first true realization of the importance of speed to market, and forget the conventional wisdom and conventional research modus operandi, was the launch of the Ford Mustang led by Lee Iacocca in 1964. From concept to "in the showroom" in seventeen months – a fraction of the time it normally took to launch new metal.

If Iacocca had taken the traditional route to the showroom Ford would have missed the sweet spot in time and customer demand and not had the most successful vehicle launch in automotive history.

In his book *The Invisible Touch* Harry Beckwith notes that people who know they are being studied change what they do. Research changes its own results. There's even a name for the above phenomenon in physics, the Heisenberg uncertainty principle, which in lay terms means that the position of the observer changes what is being observed. Too often research is used for the wrong thing, like covering your ass with the board or your boss. Too often the result of expensive, time-consuming, decision delaying research at best is not socialized effectively or at worst is misleading.

Anyone in any retail organization who suggests research without an action plan of what to do with the information discovered should be fired.

One of the things that is tough to deal with in research is attitude versus behaviour. Ask a person in a focus group if they would purchase a product with environmentally friendly packaging versus the standard eco-unfriendly packaging and overwhelmingly they will tell you they would. However, if you put the same people in a store in front of a product with eco-friendly packaging and a traditionally packaged product that costs half as much, which do you think they're more likely to pick?

The fast food industry took some serious missteps due to research. Attitudinally people in general are more health conscious but behaviourally the vast majority of Wendy's customers are not rushing there for a double salad sprinkled with lemon juice, if you get my drift. Research says, "People want to eat healthy so let's spend heavy to accommodate this attitude." The customer standing in front of the counter says, "I'd like a double bacon cheese burger, large fries, and a jumbo Coke, please."

Through years and years of experience working with the first, second, or third largest retailer in just about every retail category and being privy to all the research I have found that research often supports okay ideas but kills great ones.

There is an example in Beckwith's book (a great read by the way) that you may have heard of which discusses an imaginary focus group conducted in Burbank, California, in 1952. A facilitator engages the eight participants in ice-breaking questions then poses the question of the day.

"Imagine an enormous park. In the center, picture a four-story medieval castle with turrets, painted a soft blue.

"Leading up to the castle, imagine a wide street with stores on either side; imagine a perfect small American town in 1915 – except that these stores are immaculate, freshly painted, and about two-thirds the size of a normal building.

"As you walk down the street, people in Goofy and Mickey Mouse costumes walk up to you and greet you happily. In various parts of the park, you find a ride through a jungle, a submarine trip, cars that race around a track and other rides.

"Would you be interested in such a park?

"Would you fly two thousand miles to visit it?

"Would you pay a hundred dollars a day for your family to visit it?"

Almost certainly, the answers to those three questions would have been maybe, no, and absolutely not. And Disneyland and Disney World might never have been built.

(In this example) we spend our hypothetical time and money in a much different way than how we spend real time and money.

I have an example much closer to home, from the iconic Hudson's Bay Company, which founded in 1670 remains North America's oldest company.

It's public knowledge that some years ago HBC spent many tens of millions of dollars developing a business platform they called the "continuum." The concept was about owning customers through various stages and socio/psychological demographics through their various storefronts, Zellers and the Bay mostly.

Research showed that it all made sense attitudinally. So the entire way the organization did business was changed. HBC was grafted onto everything. However the consumer did not give a damn about HBC. Their store was the Bay or Zellers and sometimes they would cross over but on their terms for their own reasons. HBC even had consultants search for the equivalent of the Nike Swoosh when they already had it in the Hudson's Bay Point Blanket/Coat Colours, literally the number one visual icon in Canadian retail – and maybe after the 2010 Olympics the number one retail visual icon in the world.

Attitudinally there was "continuum" but behaviourally primary Zellers customers in general did not want to pay Bay prices and the Bay primary customers in general did not want Zellers fashion or brand.

I've oversimplified the scenario but the research overall resulted in a very costly mistake for the Company of Adventurers. It all made sense to those outside consultants who made millions in fees and it did fulfill a corporate agenda but the consumer was not buying it. In the end it comes down to customers voting with their feet. Perception is reality; attitude and behaviour are often very different.

In retrospect the concept of the continuum is even more ludicrous as the Zellers chain was sold early in 2011 to Target for $1.8 billion. The continuum was truly a case of corporate agenda bullshit taking precedence over consumer agenda reality. The good news is that the Bay is back to being the single jewel in the crown of the oldest company in North America. Bonnie Brooks, president of the Bay, is doing a fabulous job. Already in just a few years she's put the Bay on the right path. It had nothing to do with the continuum but rather with things like dumping 800 irrelevant fashion brands but adding 200 relevant brands. It was about being a great merchant – and I believe Bonnie is one of the great merchants of our time – and a leader, not about wading through mind-numbing research.

Retail today more than ever before is non-forgiving. A large percentage of store brands that existed over the last decade or so don't exist today; in Canada, just in mass merchandising, Eaton's, Simpsons, Woodward's, Woolco, Towers, Kmart, and soon Zellers, are gone.

Everything has changed except the fact that all retailers are fighting for a piece of a shrinking pie and only the great will prosper.

CHAPTER 11

LESSONS LEARNED

WHEN we moved to our new offices in 1993, spread over several floors in the Padulo Building at the corner of Yonge & St. Clair in Toronto, we put ads in the nearby bus shelters that read, "Starting September 27, Yonge & St. Clair becomes Yonge & Padulo … there goes the neighbourhood."

I've learned that you can take your business seriously but you should never take yourself seriously.

As an entrepreneur I'm always afraid. You think people are going to find out that you're not that smart. Until you do things and then you think, "WOW, I did that!" Bite off more than you can chew and swallow like hell – that's always been my modus operandi. So I've learned that if I really put my mind to it, I can do just about anything.

I've worked for many many retail clients in Canada and around the world. We've also acted for such financial institutions as CIBC, Citi Cards, and President's Choice Financial; automotive companies including GM, Ford, Honda, Hyundai, Jaguar, and Suzuki; as well as cosmetic companies like Revlon and Redken and manufacturers like Simmons Mattress and Phantom Industries (hosiery); and so many more. For years we worked for the Ontario Government and various government ministries. We also worked for the Ontario Lottery and Gaming Corporation and created the *Imagine the Freedom* jingle that positioned Lotto 6/49 for many years. (Although my friend Gary Gray, one of the most brilliant, down-to-earth minds in Canadian ad history, actually coined the phrase. Gary also came up with "When you eat your Smarties, do you eat the red ones last?")

I've learned that every client I work with has something to teach me.

I've received many honours over the years, including Marketer of the Year and Entrepreneur of the Year, and Padulo Integrated was voted one of Canada's 50 Best Managed Private Companies in the inaugural year of the award.

But again not one of the honours was mine because I've learned that every award I've ever won and every success I've ever enjoyed belongs to my team; I was just the front man.

Marketer of the Year award

Entrepreneur of the Year award

50 Best Managed Companies in Canada award

The Financial Post

50

Best Managed
Companies
in Canada

CANADA

PRIME MINISTER · PREMIER MINISTRE

It is with great pleasure that I extend my greetings to everyone gathered here tonight in honour of Canada's 50 Best Managed Private Companies.

Each of these companies is a success in its own right. They are the standard-bearers for today's economy. Their accomplishments are a testament to the value of hard work, good management and that special entrepreneurial zeal that translates ideas to action.

Canada's small and medium-sized businesses are the engine that will drive our economy to future prosperity, and the companies being celebrated this evening are leading the pack. They are the best and the brightest of the thousands of enterprises that are striving to succeed in an economy brimming with challenges and opportunities.

I join the Financial Post and Arthur Andersen & Co. in congratulating Canada's 50 Best Managed Private Companies for a job very well done and offer my best wishes for continued success in all future endeavours.

Jean Chrétien

TORONTO
January 17, 1994

Although physically I feel like a kid I've been around for long enough to sometimes feel like a dinosaur. My oldest son, Rich, who I hope one day will be my successor, tells me, "Dad, you're not a dinosaur, you're frickin' Yoda"… and if that means I'm older and wiser then I guess that's true and I've learned something.

If I look at any successful campaign that I've ever been involved with they all have one thing in common and that's "the offer, the promise" that is founded in truth and is sustainable. I've learned that the most successful retailers are the ones that are always working hard to get the offer right and make it come to life at store level and at every touch point.

I've learned that:

- My clients are the smartest people in the world and I can't thank them enough for hiring me.

- We in the agency business have the far easier job; our clients have the harder job. Whether it's *Because … the Lowest Price Is the Law* for Zellers or *Black's Is Photography* for Black's or *The Don't Pay a Cent Event* for Leon's or *Seeing Beyond* for CIBC or *A Pharmacy First* for Rexall I've learned that great clients work hard to find the substantive sustainable differentiator and make sure it comes to life and is representative of their primary essence – part of their "meme," part of their core DNA.

- Helping my clients find that better offer and bring it to market in a way that their customers understand is something very meaningful that I can do to help.

- Doing the right thing is the single most important primary motivator in my business life and is at the core of any successful business.

- Life really is 10 percent what happens to you and 90 percent what you do about it, or as Woody Allen puts it, "90 percent of life is just showing up," or as my dad said, "It's how many times you get up."

With my oldest friend Murray Merkley. Our mothers used to push us in our baby carriages together. Our vehicles may have changed but the lifelong friendship remains.

- Trust and respect are at the core of every successful relationship.
- Friendship whether born in a sandbox or in a business relationship is something to be cherished forever.
- Not a second of the time you spend with your kids is wasted.
- The pendulum has swung too far when I have to bill a client for their portion of the sandwiches and Cokes served in our boardroom during a lunch meeting, or a client's assistant can't accept the dozen roses I send

her as a "petite" thank you for going out of her way for me … This just does not sit right with me.

- In retail there are three things that particularly excite customers and they are when a retailer Opens, Closes, or Renovates.

- Half price is more motivating to customers than 50 percent off.

- 60 percent of retail sales are done in the first store a client thinks of so if a retailer is not top-of-mind then it is fighting for the leftover 40 percent.

- A retailer cannot cost cut their way to success and if your year-to-year same store sales are not going up you're screwed.

- One of the first places a number-crunching retailer looks to cut costs when things are tight is advertising/marketing because it's easy to cut and tough to measure. We've all heard the expression, "I know half of my ad spend is wasted I just don't know which half." Cute phrase but dumb.

- In a soft market when times are tough and everyone is pulling back it's the retailers who stay the course and stay aggressive that are poised for the quantum leap forward when the market turns up.

- Retailers focused on last year's comparables are never going to win.

- The sum of the total really is greater than the sum of the individual parts when it comes to an ad campaign.

- The death of conventional TV advertising has been greatly exaggerated.

- The effectiveness of actually selling on the net has also been greatly exaggerated, although before you forward thinkers hang me for blaspheming let me say I do agree you have to be there and be positioned for the future.

- It's your people in the stores who are in direct contact with your customers that are the most important component of your marketing mix. You've heard it and it's true … If you are not serving a customer you better damn well be serving someone who is.

- Fiefdoms and silos in retail are always bad.

- There are only two things that I consider a firing offence: (1) speaking badly about a client and (2) political behaviour.

- We are first and foremost a high-end service company that just happens to be skilled in the advertising/marketing discipline.

- Whenever anyone I'm talking with starts a sentence with the words "with all due respect" I bloody well know I'm not going to like the next words out of their mouth.

- Every woman I've ever had a significant personal relationship with or any woman who has ever had a senior role in any of my companies is smarter than me … It's an addendum to Murphy's Law.

- Good relationships go both ways and we truly do reap what we sow.

- Perception is reality.

- A good plan that is fanatically integrated and executed is better than a great plan that isn't.

- And finally I've learned that good listening is always more important than good talking.

If you can keep your head when all about you
Are losing theirs and blaming it on you,
If you can trust yourself when all men doubt you,
But make allowance for their doubting too;
If you can wait and not be tired by waiting,
Or being lied about, don't deal in lies,
Or being hated, don't give way to hating,
And yet don't look too good, nor talk too wise:

If you can dream ~ and not make dreams your master;
If you can think ~ and not make thoughts your aim;
If you can meet with Triumph and Disaster
And treat those two impostors just the same;
If you can bear to hear the truth you've spoken
Twisted by knaves to make a trap for fools,
Or watch the things you gave your life to, broken,
And stoop and build 'em up with worn-out tools:

If you can make one heap of all your winnings
And risk it on one turn of pitch-and-toss,
And lose, and start again at your beginnings
And never breathe a word about your loss;
If you can force your heart and nerve and sinew
To serve your turn long after they are gone,
And so hold on when there is nothing in you
Except the Will which says to them: 'Hold on!'

If you can talk with crowds and keep your virtue,
Or walk with Kings ~ nor lose the common touch,
if neither foes nor loving friends can hurt you,
If all men count with you, but none too much;
If you can fill the unforgiving minute
With sixty seconds' worth of distance run,
Yours is the Earth and everything that's in it,
And ~ which is more ~ you'll be a Man, my son!

Rudyard Kipling

CHAPTER 12

EVEN THE FUTURE AIN'T WHAT IT USED TO BE

HOW many times have we all heard the expression (usually after a particularly bad episode in life) that what doesn't kill you makes you stronger. Well sometimes I wish I wasn't so strong.

I've been in the business a lot of years and I've been through a lot of crap. I would scream and yell and fall down and not want to talk to anybody and crawl into a hole filled with self-pity … but only for about a day and a half. Then I'd come back swinging and I'm here to tell you that if I can do it anyone can. I may be the poster boy for "if he can do it anyone can."

I remember playing football in college and winning player of the week honours two weeks in a row; once for offence, once for defence.

My coach is congratulating me in front of the whole team and says, "Look what Padulo did and with his ability…"

To this day I don't know whether to revere that coach or hate him but I choose to believe that what he was saying was make the best of what you've got.

He used to tell me, "Padulo you're small but you're slow too."

But it didn't matter and he knew it because he knew me as a person. If he complimented me I tried harder to get better and prove him right; if he crapped on me I tried harder to get better and prove him wrong.

Whatever anyone has ever said or done to me has been motivational to me.

In my office I have hanging behind my desk the Rudyard Kipling Poem "IF" because it is a constant reminder of the traits you must emphasize to succeed.

Everything old is new again. Kipling's words applied nearly 120 years ago are relevant today and will resonate far into the future.

Even the future ain't what it used to be or is it?

- *I believe always doing the right thing will always be the right thing to do.*

- *It's the technical things that change through science and technology not our raison d'être.*

- *We all know that the sum total of human knowledge is now doubling every year and we can watch revolutions in real time.*

- *We all know that the Net has changed almost everything.*

- *We all know that our mobile phones are a magic wand … that everything we want or need is going to be on our mobile device: research, knowledge, debit, credit, loyalty points, payments, communication. And that's just scratching the surface; wait until you see what's going to happen in the next five years. The social network Facebook*

*has more than 800 million users today so yes the only
constant is change.*

But what hasn't changed and what I think will never
change is our humanity.

There is something strangely human about personal
contact, about family, about friendship, about the things that
transcend our lives.

On April 6, 2006, I lost my middle son, Alex. Alex was
in the Canadian Armed Forces, Third Royal Canadian
Regiment. As a General who spoke at Alex's memorial put
it, "Alex was a silver bullet destined to succeed in anything
he did."

But it wasn't his brains or his physical prowess (although
Alex had an abundance of both), it was Alex's humanity that
set him apart. Chris Stoiles, Alex's best army buddy, spoke
at Alex's memorial. Chris did not mention the fact that Alex
had won an Achievement Award for being the fittest guy in
the regiment, which Alex had done. Chris told a story about
one of Alex's friends collapsing on a forced march (with
compulsory time or failure component) with knapsacks and
rifles with a few miles to go.

Alex knew his friend would surely miss his time and
fail. So he went back, picked up his friend's knapsack and
rifle and basically carried him to the finish line in the time
required for both of them to stay in the unit. Being fit is a
good achievement but having the humanity to use that
strength to help a friend, even at your own peril, is a great
achievement.

Alex's strength is a beacon for us. All the little tragedies
that befall us in life and business pale in comparison with
the loss of Alex. But now anytime something good happens

we celebrate Alex. Anytime something bad happens we say this is nothing compared with ...

My friend Brian Seater sent me an e-mail after Alex's death with a copy of an article that ran in the *Houston Chronicle* that helped put things in perspective for me. The implication was obvious, the lesson was understood.

On Nov. 18, 1995, Itzhak Perlman, the violinist, came on stage to give a concert at Avery Fisher Hall at Lincoln Center in New York City. If you have ever been to a Perlman concert, you know that getting on stage is no small achievement for him. He was stricken with polio as a child, and so he has braces on both legs and walks with the aid of two crutches.

To see him walk across the stage one step at a time, painfully and slowly, is an unforgettable sight. He walks painfully, yet majestically, until he reaches his chair. Then he sits down, slowly, puts his crutches on the floor, undoes the clasps on his legs, tucks one foot back and extends the other foot forward. Then he bends down and picks up the violin, puts it under his chin, nods to the conductor and proceeds to play.

By now, the audience is used to this ritual. They sit quietly while he makes his way across the stage to his chair. They remain reverently silent while he undoes the clasps on his legs. They wait until he is ready to play.

But this time, something went wrong. Just as he finished the first few bars, one of the strings on his violin broke. You could hear it snap – it went off like gunfire across the room. There was no mistaking what that sound meant. There was no mistaking what he had to do.

People who were there that night thought to themselves: "We figured that he would have to get up, put on the clasps again, pick up the crutches and limp his way off stage – to either find another violin or else find another string for this one."

But he didn't. Instead, he waited a moment, closed his eyes and then signaled the conductor to begin again. The orchestra began, and he played from where he had left off.

And he played with such passion and such power and such purity as they had never heard before. Of course, anyone knows that it is impossible to play a symphonic work with just three strings. I know that, and you know that, but that night Itzhak Perlman refused to know that. You could see him modulating, changing, recomposing the piece in his head.

At one point, it sounded like he was de-tuning the strings to get new sounds from them that they had never made before. When he finished, there was an awesome silence in the room. And then people rose and cheered. There was an extraordinary outburst of applause from every corner of the auditorium. We were all on our feet, screaming and cheering, doing everything we could to show how much we appreciated what he had done.

He smiled, wiped the sweat from his brow, raised his bow to quiet us, and then he said, not boastfully, but in a quiet, pensive, reverent tone, "You know, sometimes it is the artist's task to find out how much music you can still make with what you have left."

What a powerful line that is. It has stayed in my mind ever since I heard it. And who knows? Perhaps that is the way of life – not just for artists but for all of us. Here is a man who has prepared all his life to make music on a violin of four strings, who, all of a sudden, in the middle of a concert, finds himself with only three strings. So he makes music with three strings, and the music he made that night with just three strings was more beautiful, more sacred, more memorable, than any that he had ever made before, when he had four strings.

So, perhaps our task in this shaky, fast-changing, bewildering world in which we live is to make music, at first with all that we have, and then, when that is no longer possible, to make music with what we have left.

Alex's death has changed me forever and I will never get over it but I have learned to live with it. I choose to go on living rather than go on dying and every day I celebrate the good things I have like my sons Rich and Shaun who

Charles Alexander Padulo with Charlie Ronalds, Alex's namesake.
Both born on November 14. Sadly, both died too early.

stood with me when I told the Itzhak Perlman story at Alex's funeral.

It was particularly poignant that there were only three of us where there had been four. But as Rich, Shaun, and I stood shoulder to shoulder we realized that if it's possible we are even closer now than before. It's Alex's fault and that's just the way Alex would want it.

I remember how Alex would tap his heart and say to his mother Joan, "I've had you up to here!"

I remember how Alex came home on leave, walked in the door, rushed over to me, grabbed me, and shook me like a rag doll, then said, "Miss you, love you," then dropped me to the floor and headed for the fridge.

A glorious ritual and a memory I will always cherish.

Shaun (left), Alex, Rich, and me.

Your family and your friendships – in the end that's really all you've got. You've got to fight for both because relationships don't always come easy but it is always your choice to nurture them.

It seems there's always something to fight for.

In 2010 I was diagnosed with prostate cancer and completed nine weeks of radiation treatment five days a week and it seems I've beat it. Like I've said before, "I'm a survivor – they'll never get me."

Well at least not for a while yet I hope!

However, when the time comes I've already written my eulogy, which I've asked Rich and Shaun to deliver at one last Rick Padulo bash. It starts out with the words,

"I always knew it would end like this ..."

My sons Rich (left), Shaun, and Alex.

My dad's baby sister Adlina (left), my dad Frank,
and his older sister Conchetta.

With Charlie Callas on a shoot for Zellers.

With Senator Art Eggleton at a launch celebration.

A gang of Paduloites at a twenty-four-hour charity run. That's Charlie Cleghorn in the middle showing off the inscription we had on all of our runners' T-shirts: the word "Padulo" followed by "we are behind you all the way."

Buddies celebrating: Holding onto Peter Thomson are Michael Murphy (left), Al Carbone, me, and Marty O'Neill. Uncle Peter is Godfather to my first-born, Rich, and I am Godfather to his first-born, Monique. We were also together the nights they were born.

With my dear friends Karen Kain and Ross Petty.

The Zellers management team at the opening
celebration of the first Padulo Building.

Uncle Marty and Alex.

The Padulo boys: (back) Jos, Dad, and me; (front) Alex, Shaun, and Rich.

Brother Jos and my beautiful (inside and out)
daughter-in-law Natasha at her wedding to Rich.

Celebrating the Grand Opening of Bar 603, which I built on one of the terraces at my condo. Some of my guests thought they were going to an actual bar opening right up to when they arrived. What a hoot!

Me dancing with Karen Kain. Can you dig it?

PADULO-O-O-OH... WHAT A NIGHT!

• JOIN RICK FOR HIS GRAND OPENING OF BAR 603
• THURSDAY JULY 23 • 7:00 PM

With Senator Art Eggleton (left), Steve Hudson, Camille Bacchus Eggleton, Neil Fedun, and Steve Kaszas.

With Clare Copeland (left), Pauline Peng-Skinner, and Fotini Copeland.

Bar 603 patio.

With Ryan Cornell (left), George Heller, Warren Jeffrey, and Andy Giancamilli.

With Linda Heller (left), Connie Leon, Nancy Jeffrey, and Wanda Giancamilli.

With Liberty Silver – she sings like an angel and her band regularly plays at my private parties.

Comedian Mike Bullard and my son Rich.

With my lifelong friends Ali, Cathy, and dad David Boydell. Ali interned for me at Padulo but was born into this world prematurely. Cathy called me and although David was not with me I was able to track him down at one of our haunts and get him to the hospital on time.

Osso Bucco dinner party at Casa Padulo, October 25, 2011, celebrating the completion of the writing of this book. (Clockwise from top) Mike Harris, Paul Godfrey, me, Dr. Stephen Small, Steve Hudson, Laura Harris, Deanna Small, Elizabeth Baszis, Wai Yi Lam, and Gina Godfrey.

With Rollie and Al Flood enjoying a great read.

(Top down) Jos' boys Chris and Greg, my son Rich,
Mummy, Jos, and me at a backyard party.

My favourite picture of Alex. We call it The Look.

INDEX

Note: Locators in italics refer to photos or photo captions.

INDEX

INDEX

INDEX

INDEX

INDEX

All proceeds from this book go to
the Alex Padulo Memorial Foundation